D0699137

THE NEW YORK PUBLIC LIBRARY'S

Books
of the
Century

THE NEW YORK PUBLIC LIBRARY'S

Books
of the
Century

Edited by ELIZABETH DIEFENDORF

Illustrations by Diana Bryan

BARNES & NOBLE

NEW YORK

Contents

Acknowledgments

The exhibition *Books of the Century,* upon which this book is based, was curated by Elizabeth Diefendorf, the Frederick Phineas and Sandra Priest Rose Chief Librarian of the General Research Division, with the assistance of librarians throughout The New York Public Library:

Robert Armitage

Gerard Belliveau

Louise Bergstresser

Neil J. Bindelgass

Stewart Bodner

Zenos Booker

Lisa Browar

Benjamin Burck

Ruth Ann Carr

Kay Cassell

Hung-Yun Chang

Nathaniel Crossland

Julie Cummins

William Cwalenski

Claire B. Dienstag

Alice Dowd

Robert Dumont

Cynthia Earman

Marilee Foglesong

Sibylle Fraser

Debbi Friedman

Tanya Gizdavcic

Leonard Gold

Harriet Gottfried

Miriam Gross

Catharine Halls

Ruby Hamilton

John Hawker

Denise Hibay

Ewa Jankowska

Diane Johnston

Edward Kasinec

Joan Kirwin
Tom Lucas
John Lundquist
Lucy E. Lyons
John T. Ma
Bernice MacDonald
Miriam Mandelbaum
Gerard Mueller
Francis W. Parr
Rodney Phillips
Susanne Pichler
Susan Pine
Warren Platt
Leacy Prior
John Rathé
Robin Rucker

Alison Ryley
Carrie Schadle
Brita Servaes
Barbara Shapiro
Anne Skillion
David Smith
Bosiljka Stevanovic
Dan Tierney
Tom Troppe
Stephen Trumble
Julia Van Haaften
Bonnie Williams
Catherine Woesthoff
Philip Yockey
Natalia Zitzelsberger

The exhibition *Books of the Century* was made possible by Reliance Group Holdings, Inc.

The New York Public Library wishes to thank the following for making the Centennial Celebration possible: Pinewood Foundation, The Freedom Forum, The New York Times Company Foundation, Inc., CIBC Wood Gundy, and Barnes and Noble, Inc.

In addition, Centennial exhibitions and programs are supported with public funds from the Cultural Challenge Initiative, a joint program of the New York State Council on the Arts, a state agency, and the New York City Department of Cultural Affairs.

THE NEW YORK PUBLIC LIBRARY'S

Books of the Century

INTRODUCTION

he New York Public Library's Books of the Century grew out of an exhibition created to celebrate the Centennial of The New York Public Library. One of many events, publications, and displays that marked our anniversary year, the exhibition drew on the enthusiasm and love of books as well as the special expertise of the institution's librarians. This little volume is permanent documentation of our effort.

The world was very different in May 1895, when The New York Public Library was founded, formed by the consolidation of the Astor Library and Lenox Library, both privately owned, and the Tilden Trust, a legacy of Samuel J. Tilden, a former governor of New York state. The site at 42nd Street and Fifth Avenue, where the great marble Library building would rise, was still occupied by the looming Croton Reservoir, a masterpiece of 19th-century architecture and hydraulic engineering, which supplied

water to the households and businesses of much of Manhattan. Horse-drawn omnibuses carried passengers up and down Fifth Avenue past churches and mansions. In 1895, patents were registered for automobiles, moving-pictures, and wireless communication. American women had 25 years to wait for the right to vote. James Joyce was 13 years old; Mao Zedong was 2. Today, most of Fifth Avenue's mansions and many of its churches are gone, and the famous thoroughfare is choked with bus and automobile traffic. Within the Library and without, text, sound, graphics, and even moving images are communicated electronically from desktop to desktop. Women are increasingly elected to political office. Joyce's Modernism has given way to Post-Modernism. An aggressive state capitalism has emerged in Mao's People's Republic of China.

Identifying books that would recall this past century and its tremendous changes was a formidable task. All

librarians on staff, whether employed in one of the four centers of The Research Libraries (which together preserve and make accessible over 50 million items) or in The Branch Libraries (which lend almost 12 million books a year in 82 neighborhood branches), were asked to suggest books that had had a significant influence, consequence, or resonance during the Library's first 100 years. Lists and ideas poured in. Many contributions came from bibliographers with substantial expertise in particular subject areas. There were lists featuring business titles, Scandinavian imprints, religious writings, historiography, Latin American literature, and science fiction. Books by suffragists, sociologists, and environmentalists all found advocates. In the end, more than 1,100 individual titles were recommended, with Upton Sinclair's *The Jungle* and Sigmund Freud's *The Interpretation of Dreams* receiving the greatest number of individual recommendations.

The exhibition opened on Centennial Day, May 20, 1995, displaying 159 works, selected from the titles recommended by librarians. To give structure to the show, the books were grouped within 11 categories — "Landmarks of Modern Literature," "Nature's Realm," and "War, Holocaust, Totalitarianism," among others — developed to acknowledge and express the artistic achievements, cataclysmic events, and intellectual trends that characterized the Library's first century. These categories have become the chapters in this book. Artist Diana Bryan was commissioned to create special murals for the exhibit, featuring cut-out silhouettes representing her interpretations of some of the books included; these have also been incorporated here.

Because we sought to engage on-site visitors in a dialogue, a very important component of the exhibit was a place for reflection, where people were invited to comment and to suggest titles they thought had played a defining role during the past 100 years. Four months into the exhibit, six notebooks were full to bursting with thoughtful reflections, some criticism, more praise, many, many interesting suggestions of individual titles to add, and plenty of heated discussion related to the issue of "political correctness." Comments ranged from "It's all a little white, male and ethnocentric, eh?" to "Excellent work, I like the breadth, lack of elitism, and inclusion of non-English titles" to "Not enough women, no lesbians. ... Why emphasize the significance of the ruling class?" to "A provocative idea—only couldn't you do another one on silenced voices?"

Several visitors commented on the issue of standards. "The choices are arbitrary and no criteria are given for them," wrote one anonymous individual, who apparently supposed that we could define an objective, quantifiable set of tests that only great books could pass. In truth, we worked with only two limits, neither of them a rule pertaining to intrinsic merit. First, because we were celebrating the Library's Centennial, a book's first appearance in print had to have fallen between 1895 and 1995 (hence no *Communist Manifesto, The Origin of Species,* or any book by Mark Twain). Second, we decided that an author could be represented by only one title (since James Joyce's *Ulysses* was in the show, his *Finnegans Wake* was not).

Another viewer grumbled, "heavily feminist...and why Stephen King?... is popularity the only criterion?" And although popularity was by no means the sole guide, neither, in every case, was literary merit or aesthetic originality. Thus, along with such universally recognized literary masterpieces as Franz Kafka's *Die Werwandlung (The Metamorphosis)* and Virginia Woolf's *To the Lighthouse,* we included classics of genre literature such as Edgar Rice Burroughs's *Tarzan of the Apes* and a "potboiler," Grace Metalious's *Peyton Place.* We also chose to exhibit some books that had, we believed, exerted a profound or lasting influence even when they were poorly written or when that influence was almost wholly evil, such as Adolf Hitler's *Mein Kampf* or Mao Zedong's *Quotations from Chairman Mao.*

Some titles included here might not even seem to be "books" at all. Neither the *United Nations Charter* nor *Smoking and Health* (known as *The Surgeon General's Report*) was first printed by a commercial publisher, but both these documents achieved wide distribution and precipitated great change.

All of us who worked on *Books of the Century* understand that any such compilation, no matter how ambitious, can only be *"Some* Books of the Century," as one visitor commented. Our choices, though certainly diverse, represent a perspective that is urban, American, and profoundly concerned with issues of social justice and freedom of expression. And ultimately there are many other books we might have included.

We have responded to the exhibition's visitors both in this book and in the exhibition itself. Many viewers had strong opinions about what we had left out; how could we have omitted Faulkner or *The Catcher in the Rye,* many of them asked. And although several children's books *were* included, many felt there should have been more, reflecting perhaps the strong attachment we all feel for the first stories and books we encounter. We have therefore added a new section, "Favorites of Childhood and Youth," which appears as the last chapter in this book. Eight other titles, including *The Portable Faulkner* and *Atlas Shrugged,* exhibited in the Library under the title "The People's Choice," have been added here to their appropriate chapters. These books are identified with the symbol ♦.

When we reflect on the response to this exhibition, what is particularly heartening to us as librarians is the strong viewer reaction. Although there is much talk today of books as an endangered species, the thoughtful and emotional reactions of so many visitors is an encouraging affirmation of the continuing importance of books to our understanding of the world. We hope that *The New York Public Library's Books of the Century* will stimulate your own reflections about the books you have read and their significance for you.

— ELIZABETH DIEFENDORF

The Frederick Phineas and Sandra Priest Rose
Chief Librarian of the General Research Division

Landmarks of
Modern Literature

One by one, the great writers most representative of the first part of this century broke with inherited traditions and remade literary forms. Novelists, especially Joyce and Woolf, experimented with stream of consciousness and interior monologue. Eliot and, later, Auden employed the rhythms of ordinary urban speech in their poetry. Pirandello overturned dramatic convention, blurring the line between actor and character. Other great writers looked back: Chekhov's three sisters, diminished and despairing, to Moscow; Proust to childhood; Yeats to

Ireland's infancy; and Millay to the traditional sonnet. After the Great Depression and the century's second global war, extraordinary writers found new language for old subjects. Nabokov produced a dark satire of sexuality and Ellison a harrowing account of marginality and rage. Writers from Latin America introduced magic realism and other playful and mythic enhancements in their fiction. The 24 writers in this section recast literature. Their books, each in its own way, confused and unsettled, challenged and renamed, echoing the turbulence of the century.

Tri sestry (1901)

{The Three Sisters}

ANTON PAVLOVICH CHEKHOV (1860–1904)

The *Three Sisters* was the first play written by Chekhov specifically for the Moscow Art Theater, where it was first performed under the direction of K. S. Stanislavsky in the winter of 1900–1901. The theme of the play—the failed struggle of an urban, cultivated family against the destructive powers of provincial banality and vulgarity —reflects the tragedy of the Russian intelligentsia of the period. Still, it retains a particular resonance in the present age. Richard Gilman writes: "*The Three Sisters* is one of the greatest of all plays, a drama as inexhaustible in its way as *Oedipus Rex* and *Hamlet* and *Lear* are in theirs."

A la recherche du temps perdu (1913–27)

{Remembrance of Things Past}

Marcel Proust (1871–1922)

An exploration of time and memory, this monumental novel is widely known for a passage in which the hero dips a madeleine into a cup of tea and is flooded with the sensations of his childhood. From this came the motif for Proust's masterpiece: "when from a long-distant past nothing subsists...the smell and taste of things remain posed a long time...and bear unfaltering, in the tiny and almost impalpable drop of their essence, the vast structure of recollection..." (from volume 1, *Swann's Way*). His novel is such a structure: the past is recovered and made permanent in one of the century's greatest literary achievements.

Tender Buttons (1914)

GERTRUDE STEIN (1874–1946)

Gertrude Stein put words to work in new ways. Interested in their melody and color, she favored verbs and prepositions in unusual combinations. "In *Tender Buttons* and then on I struggled with the ridding of myself of nouns," she explained in one of her "Lectures in America." "I knew that nouns must go...if anything that is everything was to go on meaning something."

Two generations of writers, including Hemingway, Fitzgerald, Ellison, and Sherwood Anderson, sat in Stein's Paris salon discussing writing. Anderson wrote that *Tender Buttons* "gives words an oddly new intimate flavor and at the same time makes familiar words seem almost like strangers....For me the work of Gertrude Stein consists in a rebuilding, an entire new recasting of life, in the city of words."

Stein's work is often compared to music and the Cubist images of her friend Pablo Picasso.

Die Verwandlung (1915)

{The Metamorphosis}

Franz Kafka (1883–1924)

In *The Metamorphosis*, Gregor Samsa awakens one morning to find himself transformed into a gigantic insect. Born in Prague of German-Jewish parents, Franz Kafka told his bizarre tale of nightmarish isolation and entrapment in a detached, objective, almost reportorial style. While critics have interpreted this chilling story variously as a description of despair in a meaningless world, as a reaction to institutional authoritarianism, and as an expression of conflict between the author and his father, its power seems to rest in its resistance to explanation.

W. H. Auden has said of it: "Had one to name the author who comes nearest to bearing the same kind of relation to our age as Dante, Shakespeare and Goethe bore to theirs, Kafka is the first one would think of."

Renascence and Other Poems (1917)

EDNA ST. VINCENT MILLAY (1892–1950)

As modernist writers exploded the rules of inherited forms, Edna St. Vincent Millay returned to traditional English versification, and gave it new life. In Millay's hands, the sonnet conveyed both a lover's longing and feminist independence; both sensual beauty and modern wit; both mystical rebirth and days in Greenwich Village. As Elizabeth Perlmutter puts it, Millay "became virtually a crusader in the reclamation of the short lyric poem from its temporary submersion in the twin sloughs of Victorian sentiment and modernist gloom."

Millay was 20 when the title poem of this volume appeared to critical and popular acclaim. Although she went on to write plays, varied verse, and works of social agitation, Millay remains best known for the melancholy beauty of her early work.

The Wild Swans at Coole (1917)

WILLIAM BUTLER YEATS (1865–1939)

By 1917, William Butler Yeats was famed for the beauty of his verse and for his devotion to Irish politics, culture, and lore. Facing disillusionment and middle age, however, he rejected his earlier efforts at lyricism and drama and turned to a new "vision." Linking a metaphysical system with symbolism, regular meter, and a colloquial idiom, Yeats established his mature voice with *The Wild Swans at Coole.*

Writes T. S. Eliot: "[To] have accomplished what Yeats did in the middle and later years is a great and permanent example — which poets-to-come should study with reverence — of what I have called Character of the Artist: a kind of moral, as well as intellectual, excellence." Yeats's poetic career spanned five decades, earning him the Nobel Prize in Literature in 1923.

Sei personaggi in cerca d'autore (1921)

{Six Characters in Search of an Author}

LUIGI PIRANDELLO (1867–1936)

The first performance of *Six Characters in Search of an Author* in 1922 in Rome outraged its audience with an irreverent premise: the play's six characters are in conflict with the actors who play their roles. The success of the play in attacking the deceptions of realism and dramatizing ideas about the nature of truth and illusion scandalized many contemporary theatre-goers and soon made Pirandello internationally famous. *Six Characters* was the first in a series of his plays that had a revolutionary influence on a new generation of dramatists, including Samuel Beckett and Eugène Ionesco.

The Nobel Prize in Literature was awarded to Pirandello in 1934 for "his bold and ingenious revival of dramatic and scenic art."

The Waste Land (1922)

T(homas) S(tearns) Eliot (1888–1965)

"The terrible dreariness of the great modern cities is the atmosphere in which 'The Waste Land' takes place," wrote Edmund Wilson in 1931. Wilson was one of the first to unravel Eliot's long landmark poem, which visited not only modern cities but medieval legend, six languages, and three dozen other writers. Rich in scholarliness and spare in hope, *The Waste Land* presented "a heap of broken images" of drought, "memory and desire" to readers fresh from a world war. In Wilson's words, the poem "enchanted and devastated a whole generation."

V. S. Pritchett described Eliot as "a trim anti-Bohemian with black bowler and umbrella...ushering us to our seats in hell." Eliot, as influential a critic as he was a poet, received the Nobel Prize in Literature in 1948.

Ulysses (1922)

James Joyce (1882–1941)

In the 1920s, U.S. customs officials sought alcohol and contraband sheets of James Joyce's new novel, published in Paris and smuggled in piecemeal by thrillseekers and literati alike. Successful smugglers found a kaleidoscopic day in the life of Leopold Bloom, rendered in frank "stream of consciousness." Many called the novel modern; the law called it obscene.

The 1933 decision of Judge John Woolsey to lift the ban on *Ulysses* marks a legal watershed, as well as a rare instance of judicial literary criticism. Describing *Ulysses* as "brilliant and dull, intelligible and obscure by turns," Woolsey credited "Joyce's sincerity and his honest effort to show exactly how the minds of his characters operate." The judge added: "In respect of the recurrent emergence of the theme of sex in the minds of his characters, it must always be remembered that his locale was Celtic and his season Spring."

Der Zauberberg (1924)

{The Magic Mountain}

Thomas Mann (1875–1955)

Thomas Mann situates his great ironic novel of ideas in a tuberculosis sanitorium high in the Swiss Alps. Here, "in the hermetic, feverish atmosphere of the enchanted mountain," engineer-hero Hans Castorp "undergoes a heightening process that makes him capable of adventures in sensual, moral, intellectual spheres, he would never have dreamed of." The ordeal is symbolic, and Castorp and his fellow invalids enact what the author called the "inner significance of the pre-war period of European history." The seductions of disorder, irrationality, and death pave the route to knowledge, health, and life.

Mann approached the novel like a symphony, working his themes in counterpoint and translating the musical leitmotiv into language. For this reason, he urged his readers to read *The Magic Mountain* twice in order to "really penetrate and enjoy its musical association of ideas." He was awarded the Nobel Prize in Literature in 1929.

The Great Gatsby (1925)

F. Scott Fitzgerald (1896–1940)

Flappers, bootleggers, lawn parties, and "crack-ups" — the stuff of F. Scott Fitzgerald's life and fiction would define the 1920s as America's "Jazz Age." Early critics called his best-selling work "second rate," and when he died his books were out of print. But time has lifted Fitzgerald's third novel out of its period and into the national consciousness.

Pursuing his lost love Daisy, Jay Gatsby invents his name and swindles a fortune. While parties fill his Long Island mansion, he stares across the water to the green light of Daisy's dock, dreaming of recapturing a mythic past. "Gatsby believed in the green light," says narrator Nick Carraway, "the orgastic future that year by year recedes before us." Writes Lionel Trilling: "Gatsby, divided between power and dream, comes inevitably to stand for America itself."

To the Lighthouse (1927)

VIRGINIA WOOLF (1882–1941)

Virginia Woolf wanted to capture the freedom and heterogeneity of psychic life, what she called "the real spirit we live by." In *To the Lighthouse,* she used the multiple consciousnesses of her characters and passages contrasting interior and exterior time, among other innovative techniques, to create a penetrating novel about the relations between men and women, and about time and death.

A growing body of criticism from recent decades has rescued *To the Lighthouse,* and the rest of Woolf's work, from dismissal by a long line of baffled commentators who typically found her work overly personal and artificial, rather than, as many would agree today, original and perceptive. Hermione Lee has said of Woolf: "the determined pursuit of control and authenticity...invigorates even the slightest of her work, and makes her major achievements solid with integrity and rich with inventiveness."

Primer romancero gitano (1928)
{Gypsy Ballads}

Federico García Lorca (1898–1936)

García Lorca is the best-known Spanish poet of the 20th century. This collection of 18 poems, commonly entitled *Romancero gitano* since the third edition, remains his most popular and appealing work. In his hands, the traditional ballad evokes the world of Andalusia and the gypsy — his culture, language, joy, and suffering — to great dramatic and lyric effect.

The author himself said of the *Gypsy Ballads:* "It is there that my poetic face appears for the first time with its own personality, well sketched and virgin of contact with any other poet."

Native Son (1940)

RICHARD (NATHANIEL) WRIGHT
(1908–1960)

"The day *Native Son* appeared," wrote Irving Howe, "American culture was changed forever." The first widely successful novel by an African American, *Native Son* shattered the myth that the descendants of slaves were "patient or forgiving," in Howe's words. "A blow at the white man, the novel forced him to recognize himself as an oppressor," wrote Howe. "A blow at the black man, the novel forced him to recognize the cost of his submission."

Bigger Thomas is poor, black, and resentful. When he accidentally kills a white woman, he accepts the role of murderer as one of the few a racist society allows him. Although Wright wanted his violent novel to arouse more anger than tears, David Bradley wrote in 1986, "I hope we have come far enough by now to read *Native Son* and weep."

The Portable Faulkner (1946)˙

WILLIAM FAULKNER (1897–1962)

No omission from *Books of the Century* caused as much indignation as did the absence of any book by William Faulkner. Rather than limit ourselves to one work by this prolific writer, we have chosen *The Portable Faulkner,* published in 1946, at a time when Faulkner's mostly out-of-print fiction was dismissed by influential critics as macabre or perverse, and when he was unhappily earning his living as a Hollywood screenwriter.

Instead of compiling a traditional anthology, editor Malcolm Cowley (with Faulkner's close collaboration) assembled a chronological mosaic of Yoknapatawpha County from elements of ten books. The reconfigured narrative begins with a Chickasaw named "Doom," "a dispossessed American king...who granted out of his lost domain a solid square mile of virgin north Mississippi dirt," and concludes with the elegiac "Delta Autumn," a story about a hunting trip in 1940 which serves as a lament for a lost paradisal wilderness.

The appearance of this volume brought about a reassessment of Faulkner's unique literary achievement, which led to his 1949 Nobel Prize in Literature.

The Age of Anxiety:
A Baroque Eclogue (1947)

W(ystan) H(ugh) Auden (1907–1973)

With his Pulitzer Prize–winning poem *The Age of Anxiety*, Anglo-American poet W. H. Auden not only captured the spirit of wartime New York City but gave the name to an era. Portraying the interior lives of four city dwellers who come together in a bar and in a West Side apartment on a night in 1944, Auden dramatized each one's personal isolation and the disquiet of the times.

Fellow poet Marianne Moore called the poem "a deep and fearless piece of work."

En attendant Godot (1952) *
{Waiting for Godot; A Tragicomedy in Two Acts}

SAMUEL BECKETT (1906–1989)

Born a Protestant in Dublin, Samuel Beckett gravitated as a young man to Paris, where he joined a coterie of French intellectuals and lively, impoverished Irish expatriates. These included James Joyce and his wife, Nora, who half-adopted Beckett. He, in turn, provided the couple with many services, such as reading aloud to Joyce after his eyesight failed. The two writers are forever canonically linked, because of their friendship, and as great masters of literary experimentation.

This play, first performed in Paris in 1952, places two Chaplinesque tramps in a barren landscape. Their fitful, fragmented conversations with each other and with the tyrant Pozzo defined the Theatre of the Absurd for postwar audiences and intellectuals. Brooks Atkinson said of an early production: "It gave a frightening impression of being close to the truth of the human race waiting indolently for a salvation that will never come."

Samuel Beckett was awarded the Nobel Prize in Literature for 1969.

Invisible Man (1952)

Ralph Ellison (1914–1994)

From an underground cell ablaze with 1,369 lightbulbs and the music of Louis Armstrong, the nameless narrator of Ralph Ellison's only novel recounts his search for identity in a hostile world. In a voice at once comic, mythic, literary, and searing, the narrator retraces his journey from South to North, innocence to experience, and naive confidence to ironic acceptance of his *lack* of identity as a black man in white America.

"I wasn't, and am not, *primarily* concerned with injustice, but with art," Ellison told an interviewer. He added, "Now, mind, I recognize no dichotomy between art and protest." To structure his novel, Ellison drew on sources ranging from Dostoevsky, Emerson, and Stein to African American folklore and jazz. *Invisible Man* won the National Book Award in 1952.

Lolita (1955)

Vladimir Nabokov (1899–1977)

"The filthiest book I have ever read. Sheer unrestrained pornography," fumed John Gordon of the London *Sunday Express* after Graham Greene had praised *Lolita* in the *Sunday Times*. As American publishers of the early 1950s would have nothing to do with a novel whose protagonist was an obsessional pedophile, Nabokov had turned to Maurice Girodias and his slightly unsavory Olympia Press to get the book published, in Paris, in the now-famous olive green covers.

Several threatened and actual lawsuits later, and preceded by publication of a long excerpt in *Anchor Review*, the first U.S. edition gingerly appeared in August 1958. Within a month, it was a best-seller. Throbbing pubescents of all ages went in search of a dirty book and found, alas, a masterpiece.

Ficciones (1944; 2nd augmented edition, 1956)

{Fictions}

JORGE LUIS BORGES (1899–1986)

Borges's powerful influence on 20th-century literature goes far beyond the borders of Spanish and Anglo-America. A master of poetry, fiction, and prose, Borges has fascinated and maddened readers of the dozens of languages into which his works have been translated.

In *Ficciones,* a collection of short stories written during the years he served as a librarian in a small branch library, one finds complex metaphysical tales that challenge the reader's sense of reality *and* accepted fiction. Ambiguity, metaphor, and fantasy abound. The appeal of his stories, as critic Donald Leslie Shaw has noted, is in "the pleasure we get from detective stories or even crossword puzzles, that is, from problem solving." The "best stories are puzzling and teasingly demand to be 'cracked.'"

Ficciones won the Formentor International Publisher's Prize, which Borges shared with Samuel Beckett in 1961.

On the Road (1957) *

Jack Kerouac (1922–1969)

With its emphasis on travel, drug experimentation, promiscuous sex, and Asian philosophy, the Beat lifestyle of the 1950s was eagerly embraced by many and contributed to a change in the American consciousness that led directly to the counterculture movement of the 1960s. When *On the Road* was published in 1957, it was simultaneously denounced for its lack of literary merit and praised for its vivid portrayal of the "Beats." Today—still in print and possessed of a cult following — it is recognized as a literary classic that bears comparison to the works of Walt Whitman, Mark Twain, and William Faulkner.

Cien años de soledad (1967)
{One Hundred Years of Solitude}

GABRIEL GARCÍA MÁRQUEZ (b. 1928)

One Hundred Years of Solitude chronicles the life of Macondo, a fictional town based in part on García Márquez's hometown of Aracataca, Colombia, and seven generations of the founding family, the Buendías. García Márquez creates a complex world with characters and events that display the full range of human experience. For the reader, the pleasure of the novel derives from its fast-paced narrative, humor, vivid characters, and fantasy elements. In this "magic realism," the author combines imaginative flights of fancy with social realism to give us images of levitating priests, flying carpets, a four-year-long rainstorm, and a young woman ascending to heaven while folding sheets.

Winner of the Nobel Prize in Literature in 1982, Gabriel García Márquez has become a formidable influence in world literature and a widely quoted commentator on Latin American politics and culture.

Portnoy's Complaint (1969) *

PHILIP ROTH (b. 1933)

In a rage, at breakneck pace, Alexander Portnoy spews out his tale to Dr. Spielvogel. He recounts the strategies he has used in his attempts to transcend his claustrophobic upbringing in northern New Jersey. These include overachievement, empathy for the (non-Jewish) downtrodden, obsessive masturbation, and futile relationships with gentile women, whom he cannot even bear to call by their Christian names. To Portnoy's despair, his tactics have not worked.

This poignant, wildly funny novel can be seen as part and parcel of the cultural ferment and artistic experimentation which characterized 1969, the tumultuous year of its publication. At the time, the book's obscenity and perceived anti-Semitism created outrage, excitement, and tremendous sales. The book endures because of vivid characterizations, perfect-pitch capture of vernacular speech, and the pathos of its hero's predicament.

Since *Portnoy,* Philip Roth has published 18 books, including *Sabbath's Theater,* which won the National Book Award in 1995.

Song of Solomon (1977)

TONI MORRISON (b. 1931)

This complex and resonant novel is the third written by Toni Morrison, recipient of the 1993 Nobel Prize in Literature. The author's insistence on the primacy of language and of naming was the subject of her Nobel Lecture, and it is also a paramount theme of this book. Two characters, father and son, are both called "Macon Dead," a "heavy name scrawled in perfect thoughtlessness by a drunken Yankee in the Union Army." But the father believes he "had some ancestor...who had a name that was real. A name that was not a joke, nor a disguise, nor a brand name...."

In accepting her Nobel Prize, Morrison stated, "Be it grand or slender, burrowing, blasting, or refusing to sanctify, whether it laughs out loud or is a cry without an alphabet, the choice word, the chosen silence, unmolested language surges toward knowledge, not its destruction."

NATURE'S REALM

The birds and the bees may not have changed much lately, but the 20th century sees them in new ways. Scientific knowledge has become more specialized in this century of revolutionary discovery. At the same time, gifted writers and scientists — including Einstein — have worked to bring abstract ideas to an ever-widening public. Thanks to Marie Curie's pioneering work, we learned about radioactive substances, which were later used in powerful and effective cancer treatments — and in the atomic bomb. We know of DNA, the genetic template first described by Watson and Crick. We find the birds in

the field (according to Peterson's guide), follow the bees to their hives (thanks to Maeterlinck)—and see how both have been imperiled by pesticides (as Rachel Carson reported). The scientific works of enduring popularity are marked by their tone of impassioned concern for the earth and its "diversity of life," in E. O. Wilson's phrase. Ironically, some of the century's greatest advances in knowledge have led to the greatest perils to the planet. Still, if humans are not always good to the planet, its natural products aren't always good for humans—as the Surgeon General has noted.

La vie des abeilles (1901)
{The Life of the Bee}

MAURICE MAETERLINCK (1862–1949)

The Life of the Bee incorporates in its pioneer observations of animal behavior its Symbolist author's mystical and philosophical musings. For today's readers, accustomed to the more objective language of ethologists such as Konrad Lorenz, this lush prose may anthropomorphize the bees a bit too much.

Maeterlinck, who was born in Belgium, was awarded the Nobel Prize in Literature in 1911. He wrote also on the life cycle of ants (*La vie des fourmis*, 1930), but is best known for his allegorical fantasy *L'oiseau bleu* (1908; translated in 1909 as *The Blue Bird*) and the play *Pelléas et Mélisande* (1892), upon which the composer Claude Debussy based his 1902 opera.

Traité de radioactivité (1910)

{Treatise on Radioactivity}

MARIE SKLODOWSKA CURIE (1867–1934)

The achievements of Marie Curie changed basic concepts in physics, and led to a new understanding of atomic structure. Polish-born Marie Sklodowska met and married Pierre Curie in Paris, where their early joint studies of magnetism led to investigations of radioactive substances. Eventually the pair discovered and extracted two new elements, polonium and radium, from the mineral pitchblende.

Marie Curie was awarded many honors, despite the entrenched antifeminism of the period: in 1903, she, Pierre, and Henri Becquerel shared the Nobel Prize in Physics. In 1909, three years after Pierre died in an accident, she was awarded his chair in physics at the Sorbonne. In 1911, she won the Nobel Prize in Chemistry, becoming the only person ever to be awarded this prize in both physics and chemistry.

The Meaning of Relativity (1922)

ALBERT EINSTEIN (1879–1955)

"Everybody knows that Einstein did something astonishing," wrote Bertrand Russell in 1925, "but very few people know exactly what it was that he did." Russell was an early commentator on "relativity," striving to explain Einstein's new universe to the common reader. In 1921, Einstein himself joined the effort, delivering four lectures exploring his special theory of relativity (1905)—the discovery that light moves at a constant speed for any observer at any position. Concluding that both motion and time are relative to the observer, Einstein upset fundamental ideas about space, time, and, in his general theory of relativity (1915), Newtonian gravitation. With a simple equation—$E = mc^2$—Einstein linked mass and energy, a revelation that found ironic proof in the development of nuclear weapons, but that redirected modern physics. Einstein was awarded the Nobel Prize in Physics in 1921.

A Field Guide to the Birds (1934)

ROGER TORY PETERSON (b. 1908)

By the simple device of pinpointing key characteristics of each bird species in schematic drawings, American naturalist/artist/author Peterson created a bird identification system that has enabled ever-increasing numbers of enthusiastic amateurs to become knowledgeable birders. His system has helped make birdwatching one of the most popular outdoor nature activities today.

Peterson's first Field Guide was the forerunner of an entire series, including not only frequently updated guides to regional birds, but also guides to other branches of natural history. The guides have been translated into at least 12 European languages, as well as into Japanese and Chinese.

Peterson's fame as author and illustrator of the Field Guides has overshadowed his achievements as an outstanding ornithological artist.

A Sand County Almanac (1949)

ALDO LEOPOLD (1886–1948)

"There are some who can live without wild things, and some who cannot. These essays are the delights and dilemmas of one who cannot." Leopold, a conservationist and environmental authority, stated this credo in the Foreword of his posthumously published *Almanac*. His beautifully written book has inspired generations of environmentalists.

In 1935, the author bought 80 acres of exhausted and abandoned farmland in Wisconsin, complete with a broken-down shed "filled with cow manure and chicken droppings." For the next 12 years, he and his family, working on weekends, gradually restored the land to health. *A Sand County Almanac* is not only a poetic and sensitively written memoir of these years, it also encompasses Leopold's thoughts about and observations of the natural world, its wildlife, and human responsibilities toward the earth we inhabit.

Er redete mit dem Vieh, den Vögeln und den Fischen: King Solomon's Ring (1949)

{King Solomon's Ring: New Light on Animal Ways}

KONRAD Z. LORENZ (1903–1989)

The original German title of *King Solomon's Ring* derives from the legend that the biblical monarch "talked with beasts, birds, and fishes." Lorenz, an Austrian-born scientist, himself had an amazing rapport with animals. His popular account of his interactions over some 25 years with dogs, fish, Water-shrews, Greylag geese, and Jackdaws transports the reader into the fascinating world of ethology, the science of the study of animal behavior.

Lorenz's many other influential books translated from the original German into English include *On Aggression* (1966), *Studies in Animal and Human Behaviour* (1970 – 71), *Evolution and Modification of Behavior* (1965), and *The Year of the Greylag Goose* (1979).

Silent Spring (1962)

RACHEL CARSON (1907–1964)

S*ilent Spring* is an impassioned, carefully researched, and meticulously documented call to arms against the indiscriminate use of chemical insecticides and weedkillers. Its publication alerted the general public to the growing danger—known already to ecologists and conservationists—from the careless and, in many cases, egregious poisoning of the earth's soil, water, air, creatures, and plants. Carson, an aquatic biologist who was awarded a Guggenheim Fellowship in 1951, never advocated abandoning all chemical weapons against weeds and animal pests, as many in the chemical and agricultural industries claimed. Rather, she urged research into alternative methods.

Among Carson's earlier books are the poetic and acutely observed *Under the Sea Wind* (1941), *The Edge of the Sea* (1955), and the best-selling *The Sea Around U*s (1951).

Smoking and Health (*known as* The Surgeon General's Report) (1964)

In 1962, President John F. Kennedy's Surgeon General, Dr. Luther L. Terry, assembled an advisory committee of distinguished medical authorities to investigate the effects of tobacco smoking on health. The message of their *Report,* backed by extensive documentation, was unequivocal: tobacco is "a health hazard of sufficient importance in the United States to warrant appropriate remedial action" (Foreword).

The exhaustive report (387 pages of closely packed text and references, with innumerable charts and graphs) continues to influence medical thought, national and local legislation, and social behavior. One could say that it is one of the most widely quoted publications ever, cited on every cigarette package and advertisement in the United States.

The tobacco industry and its powerful lobbies continue to discount the findings of *Smoking and Health.*

The Double Helix: A Personal Account of the Discovery of the Structure of DNA (1968)

JAMES DEWEY WATSON (b. 1928)

Until the 1950s, chromosomes and genes were accepted as the basic genetic units. Then James Watson, Francis Crick, Maurice Wilkins, and other biological researchers discovered that the fundamental genetic material is DNA (deoxyribonucleic acid), whose molecule assumes the form of a double helix.

In 1962, Watson, Crick, and Wilkins were jointly awarded the Nobel Prize in Physiology or Medicine for their discovery. Nevertheless, *Honest Jim,* Watson's first draft of *The Double Helix,* was severely criticized because of the author's gratuitously negative comments about many of his colleagues. Despite major revisions by Watson, many in the scientific community remain critical.

Although DNA is not as conclusively reliable an identifier as are fingerprints, its growing acceptance as evidence in criminal and medical work has made this term a household word.

The Diversity of Life (1992)

EDWARD O. WILSON (b. 1929)

There are at least 1.82 million *known* animal and plant species (excluding fungi and one-celled creatures), and countless millions more unknown. Many of these species have already disappeared; others will disappear in the future because of natural events.

But extinctions result also from human indifference and greed, and in this eloquent book, biologist Edward Wilson speaks about such threats to the diversity of life on earth, and how this will impact humanity. Wilson focuses on the vulnerable tropical rain forests, where myriad life forms abound, describing in detail the lives of insects and other minute creatures.

Wilson won the Pulitzer Prize for general nonfiction in 1979 for *On Human Nature,* and shared it in 1991 with Bert Holldobler for *The Ants,* their study of Wilson's favorite insects.

Protest & Progress

Telling a story can change the world. The Americans who fill this section have proved as much, bringing to the page the national faith in progress and the power of the individual. In their books, words became actions. Life stories and impassioned advocacy fueled revolutions: W.E.B. Du Bois, James Baldwin, and Malcolm X all illuminate the horror of racial oppression. Hearing others' stories fired social action: Jane Addams opened her house to Chicago poor and founded modern social work; Lillian

Wald nursed the needy and launched public health. Journalists, such as the muckraker Upton Sinclair and, in our time, Randy Shilts, flung charges at industrialists and politicos — winning shocked concern. The effort to see beyond cliches led to the haunting fictions of Steinbeck and Dos Passos. Perhaps Agee voiced the fear of all artists who write to change, not to please: "Above all else: in God's name don't think of it as Art."

The Battle with the Slum (1902)

JACOB RIIS (1849–1914)

Born in Ribe, Denmark, Jacob Riis immigrated to America in 1870. By 1877 he was a police reporter for the *New York Tribune,* a job that took him into the back alleys, tenements, and "seven-cent lodging houses" of New York's most notorious slums. He was as famous for his innovations in the documentation of squalid urban conditions (he used the newly invented flashbulb to illuminate and photograph sunless interiors) as for his wide-ranging reformist zeal (he exposed the pollution of New York City's water supply and successfully advocated the purchase of the upstate Croton watershed).

His greatest concern, however, was with the corrosive effect of the brutal conditions of America's slums on suffering and defenseless individuals. In *The Battle with the Slum,* his signature work, he movingly tells many of their stories.

The Souls of Black Folk (1903)

W(illiam) E(dward) B(urghardt) Du Bois (1868–1963)

Leader and rebel, historian and prophet, W.E.B. Du Bois brought race to the center of the American consciousness. "The problem of the Twentieth Century is the problem of the color-line," he proclaimed, defying the popular rhetoric of Booker T. Washington, who urged blacks to cheerful acceptance of second-class citizenship. Throughout his long career, Du Bois persisted in confronting slavery and its lingering horrors. He demanded the vote — "else what shall save us from a second slavery?" His words wove together song, story, and scholarship, and have inspired a century of readers with their images of the "double consciousness" of black Americans living "within the Veil."

Writes John Edgar Wideman, "For the oppressed, *Souls* is a beacon, a rallying cry." Du Bois matched his words with a long career of action, including co-founding the NAACP in 1909.

The Jungle (1906)

Upton Sinclair (1878–1968)

Sinclair's best-known work, an expose of the Chicago meat-packing industry disguised as a novel, *The Jungle* caught the attention of President Theodore Roosevelt with its lurid descriptions of the conditions in which men perished and potted chicken was not potted chicken at all:

> The President wrote to me that he was having the Department of Agriculture investigate the matter, and I replied that that was like asking a burglar to determine his own guilt. If Roosevelt really wanted to know anything about conditions in the yards, he would have to make a secret and confidential investigation....The commissioners obtained evidence of practically everything charged in "The Jungle;" except that I was not able to produce legal proof of men falling into vats and being rendered into pure leaf lard.

Sinclair's graphic best-seller led Congress to establish the federal meat inspection law and the Pure Food and Drug Act.

Twenty Years at Hull-House (1910)

JANE ADDAMS (1860–1935)

Twenty Years at Hull-House is both autobiography and blueprint for social action. "I gradually became convinced," wrote Jane Addams, "that it would be a good thing to rent a house in a part of the city where many primitive and actual needs are found." Addams made these needs her life's work. For Addams, that meant living with the poor and dispossessed. The dilapidated Hull mansion on Halstead Street, in a teeming Chicago immigrant neighborhood, was the house, and its first 20 years witnessed pioneering social achievement.

In every early 20th-century public opinion poll before 1914, Jane Addams ranked as the most admired American woman, often as the most admired American. Her national esteem suffered fatally when she refused to compromise her antimilitarism in World War I. Though she continued to pursue many progressive causes, her energy increasingly focused on peace issues. In 1931, Addams was awarded the Nobel Peace Prize.

The House on Henry Street (1915)

LILLIAN WALD (1867–1940)

In 1895, the financier and philanthropist Jacob Schiff bought Lillian Wald and Mary M. Brewster a house at 265 Henry Street. The two young nurses had moved into the tenements of the Lower East Side to live among the sick and destitute. Their effort would evolve into the famous Henry Street Settlement, a center of social outreach and community involvement that introduced generations of new immigrants to American life; the Settlement remains active at the same address today, serving a different constituency but still reflecting the ideals and concerns that animated its founders. Wald herself went on to become a pioneer in public health; her promotion of nursing services in the public schools led in 1902 to the establishment by the New York City Board of Health of the first such program in the world.

The Autobiography of Lincoln Steffens (1931)

Lincoln Steffens (1866–1936)

When President Theodore Roosevelt judged that the vigorous investigative reporting of Lincoln Steffens was counterproductive and actually undermining reform, he castigated the writer as "the Man with the Muck-rake, who could look no way but downward." Thus, Steffens, as well as Ida Tarbell, Ray Stannard Baker, and others who energized American journalism in the first decade of this century, came to be known as "muckrakers."

As managing editor of *McClure's Magazine*, Steffens worked with whistle-blowing local informants to expose political corruption and graft in St. Louis, Minneapolis, Pittsburgh, Chicago, and New York. In 1904, these articles were collected and published as *The Shame of the Cities*, a book that created a national sensation. Steffens later used the same fact-finding techniques and reformist passion to explore abuses resulting from America's minimally regulated economic system. His reputation was in decline, however, in 1931, when *The Autobiography of Lincoln Steffens* appeared. Its publication regained for him both fame and respect.

U.S.A. (1937)

JOHN DOS PASSOS (1896–1970)

The *U.S.A.* trilogy, published as a single volume for the first time in 1937, is a sweeping portrayal of industrial America during the 30 years from the turn of the century to the first year of the Great Depression. The novel's experimental modes—"Newsreels," collages of headlines, song lyrics, and other bits of pop ephemera; the authorial "Camera Eye"; quirky biographical sketches of public figures; and longer fictional narratives — gave cinematic scale to its ambition.

Dos Passos's U.S.A. was a country where only the unscrupulous had any control over their lives: where everyone was on the make and greed triumphed. At the end, only a few radicals still hope for a better future. No wonder that Sartre, writing in 1938, pronounced Dos Passos "the greatest writer of our time."

The Grapes of Wrath (1939)

JOHN STEINBECK (1902–1968)

As Farm Security Administration photographs have come to define the Great Depression in images, *The Grapes of Wrath* has come to do so in words. Proletarian heroes are all but invisible in our literature today, but this proletarian novel spoke eloquently for the many "forgotten" men and women of the 1930s. It speaks to us still today.

John Steinbeck had been sent by the *San Francisco News* to investigate the living conditions of Dust Bowl emigrants then pouring into a glutted California labor market. This furnished the raw material of *The Grapes of Wrath,* the grimly realistic story of the odyssey of the Joad family, dispossessed tenant farmers, from Oklahoma to the failed promised land.

Praised and vilified alike, *The Grapes of Wrath* sold over three million copies and won the 1940 Pulitzer Prize for fiction. In 1962, to his apparent discomfort, John Steinbeck was awarded the Nobel Prize in Literature.

Let Us Now Praise Famous Men (1941)

JAMES AGEE (1909–1955)
AND WALKER EVANS (1903–1975)

In 1936, *Fortune* commissioned James Agee and photographer Walker Evans to investigate tenant farming in the Deep South. The outcome of this extraordinary collaboration, quite unacceptable to *Fortune*, was both an unsparing record of the harsh existence of three Alabama families, and a poetic meditation on the terrible beauty of their lives.

Reviewers in 1941 were puzzled or offended by the book's experimental style and heightened language. *Time* magazine quipped: "As a book, this is the most distinguished failure of the season...."

"If I could do it," Agee wrote, "I'd do no writing at all here. It would be photographs; the rest would be fragments of cloth, bits of cotton, lumps of earth, records of speech, pieces of wood and iron, phials of odors, plates of food and of excrement...nothing I might write could make any difference at all." In fact, Agee's writing, prefaced by Evans's photographs, continues to haunt.

Strange Fruit (1944)

Lillian Smith (1897–1966)

Strange Fruit is about what happens when the ritual of segregation is flouted: the love affair of an educated black woman and an unexceptional white man culminates in murder and a public lynching. Lillian Smith's novel was rejected by seven publishers before it appeared in 1944. Its popular success was at least partly due to attempts to suppress it, in the South for its message, in the North for "obscenity."

Smith lived in Georgia and was involved in "the question about race" all her life. Some 9,000 of her letters pertaining to the period when she was most active, which had been collected at the request of the Library of Congress, were destroyed, along with manuscripts and other material, when her house was burned by two white arsonists in 1955, and again in 1958.

Growing Up Absurd (1960)

PAUL GOODMAN (1911–1972)

When he died in 1972, Paul Goodman was memorialized in *The New York Times* for "the scope and scale of [his] interests, [which] can be seen in the catalogue of the New York Public Library, where his books are listed under 21 different categories, ranging from fiction to education to poetry to applied linguistics to drama to United States Constitutional law."

Novelist, poet, essayist, and lay therapist, Goodman became godfather to the 1960s counterculture. Of his prodigious output, *Growing Up Absurd* will for better or worse probably be longest remembered. Excoriating the "Organized System of semimonopolies, government, advertisers, etc." that he saw grinding down the lives of young people, he called for "radical" but "practicable" change and applauded those who dropped out of the System. The Rousseauian theme of much of his work was that humankind is essentially creative and good, while institutions and bureaucracies are repressive and bad.

The Fire Next Time (1963)

JAMES BALDWIN (1924–1987)

James Baldwin won an audience in 1953 with his semi-autobiographical novel, *Go Tell It on the Mountain.* But he made his mark on the Civil Rights generation ten years later with two scathing, sermon-like essays. In "My Dungeon Shook" and "Down at the Cross" — first published in wide-circulation magazines — Baldwin predicted apocalypse. He held out hope that, with work, "the relatively conscious whites and the relatively conscious blacks...may be able...to end the racial nightmare." But failing reconciliation, he predicted rioting, assassinations, and chaos that came eerily true the year the essays were published as *The Fire Next Time.*

Born in Harlem, Baldwin lived much of his life in France to escape racial oppression. Upon his death, Nobel laureate Toni Morrison recalled: "You made American English honest.... You stripped it of ease and false comfort and fake innocence and evasion and hypocrisy. And in place of deviousness was clarity."

The Autobiography of
Malcolm X (1965)

MALCOLM X (1925–1965)

"If you knew him you would know why we must honor
him: Malcolm was our manhood, our living, black manhood!…In honoring him, we honor the best in ourselves."
Actor/director/playwright Ossie Davis spoke those words
over Malcolm X's murdered body more than 30 years ago.
Since then, layers of myth have accrued around Malcolm's
name. His autobiography, a story of self-creation and
redemption, reveals the complicated, compelling, still-
evolving private man. Jailed for burglary, in the closed
world of prison Malcolm Little found freedom in the
power of the word. He read prodigiously; became a passionate convert to Elijah Muhammad's Black Muslim
movement; and walked out as Malcolm X. His later pilgrimage to Mecca, after his break with Elijah Muhammad, was another transforming experience. Each of these
changes was a stage in a long spiritual and intellectual
journey, uncompleted at his death.

"If I'm alive when this book comes out, it will be a
miracle," he wrote. "It's a time for martyrs now."

And the Band Played On (1987)

RANDY SHILTS (1952–1994)

"AIDS did not just happen to America," charged Randy Shilts. "It was allowed to happen." In this meticulously researched saga, Shilts traced the first five years of the AIDS epidemic in America. He blended stories of human suffering and medical sleuthing with charges of gross institutional negligence. Health care officials, the Reagan administration, individual scientists, and even gay leaders all "played politics with the disease," wrote Shilts. Delaying funding and concern, they created "a drama of national failure, played out against a backdrop of needless death."

And the Band Played On brought AIDS care to national prominence, achieving best-seller status and earning a National Book Award nomination. The book remains controversial, criticized for its overwhelming detail and blame-placing, but hailed by *The New York Times* as "a heroic work of journalism." Shilts completed *Conduct Unbecoming,* a study of gay men and lesbians in the military, before succumbing to AIDS at age 42.

There Are No Children Here (1991)

ALEX KOTLOWITZ (b. 1955?)

Almost a century after Jane Addams founded Hull-House, *Wall Street Journal* reporter Alex Kotlowitz entered the lives of two young brothers growing up in the Henry Horner Homes, an isolated Chicago housing project. Lafeyette and Pharoah Rivers live with their mother, six siblings, and other relatives in a dangerously dilapidated apartment, which lacks a telephone. The children dodge gunfire while walking to elementary school. Both fear they will not survive to adulthood.

"His great love for Pharoah and Lafeyette has transformed Kotlowitz himself into the antidote to nihilism," wrote Thomas Byrne Edsall in the *New Republic.* "How can such deep personal commitment be legislated or replicated on a vast public scale?"

In 1992, Kotlowitz was awarded The New York Public Library Helen Bernstein Award for Excellence in Journalism for this book. *There Are No Children Here* was adapted as a TV movie, produced by and starring Oprah Winfrey, which aired on ABC in 1993.

COLONIALISM & ITS AFTERMATH

In its heyday, colonialism was justified as an expanding front of civilization. Today, it suggests oppression and exploitation, and yesterday's great empires continue their retreat. Literature has played a key role in the turnaround. Colonial subjects began to speak out, reclaiming voice and autonomy. Colonists confronted their failures in accurately imagined tales of horror. The testimony of each group survives in the written word. Gandhi's newspaper columns; Rigoberta Menchú's witness to the massacre of Indians in Guatemala; Fanon's pan-African call to arms—all played active roles in strug-

gles toward independence. New novels from French Indochina, the West Indies, and Africa speak for a younger generation torn between cultures; meanwhile, epic novels of the imperial encounter live on. Talented journalists like Kapuściński have employed investigative as well as literary skills to analyze cultural change. A new world of hope and tolerance is reflected in the family portraits assembled by Steichen, and in documents like the U.N. Charter. But conflicts arise anew, and issues of colonialism have not disappeared.

Lord Jim (1900)

JOSEPH CONRAD (BORN JÓZEF TEODOR KONRAD KORZENIOWSKI) (1857–1924)

In a moment of crisis, an idealistic ship's officer abandons his post, leaving several hundred passengers to drown. The event at the center of Joseph Conrad's acclaimed novel establishes the character and fate of Jim. Tormented by his defection from his code of conduct, Jim embarks on a globe-traveling quest to regain honor. In the process, he insinuates himself as a leader among a people unaware of his past.

Arthur Symons and other critics read *Lord Jim* as an exploration of Conrad's own "ideal of an applauded heroism," an ideal that confronts the demands of pragmatism. Others see an allegory for Conrad's guilt over abandoning his native Poland or, alternatively, a story of universal shame. Conrad has come under modern attack for associating "natives" with chaos and evil. But in Conrad's novels, it is ultimately the colonial system itself that is fraught with horror.

Kim (1901)

(Joseph) Rudyard Kipling (1865–1936)

Few writers have been both as adored and as vilified as
Rudyard Kipling. Cherished by children for his vivid
"Jungle Books," Kipling also penned letters, poems,
tales, and novels that made him one of the most popular
writers of all time. But critics soon charged racism in his
depiction of colonial India, where Kipling was born to
English parents.

Kim, Kipling's final book about India, was termed
"magical" upon publication. When the orphaned Kimball
O'Hara joins a Buddhist lama in his search for the River
of Healing, the reader beholds a kaleidoscope of people
and settings through the child's wonderstruck eyes. Ben-
gali critic Niraud Chaudhuri has called *Kim* "the finest
novel in the English language with an Indian theme," but
Bhupal Singh charged, "the soul of India remains hidden
from [Kipling's] eyes." Rudyard Kipling was awarded the
Nobel Prize in Literature in 1907, the first Englishman to
be so honored.

Satyagraha [Non-Violent Resistance] (1921–40)

MOHANDAS KARAMCHAND GANDHI (1869–1948)

The great Indian philosopher and statesman Gandhi first practiced "Satyagraha," or "devotion to truth," in South Africa. Instead of attacking the Transvaal government, which in 1906 ordered all "Asiatics" to register with the police, Gandhi emphasized polite, nonviolent noncooperation. With ancient tools, Gandhi launched a modern cause.

Ten years later, Gandhi took Satyagraha to India, electrifying the nation into opposing British rule through peaceful boycotts. Later, in widely read newspaper columns, Gandhi clarified the philosophy he drew from the *Bhagavad-Gita*, Thoreau, Tolstoy, and his wife Kasturba. "A Satyagrahi will always try to overcome evil by good, anger by love, untruth by truth," he told a war-torn world. "There is no other way of purging the world of evil." Gandhi led the way to India's independence in 1947. His work would inspire Martin Luther King, Jr., and shape the century's lasting struggles against colonialism, racism, and violence.

A Passage to India (1924)

E(DWARD) M(ORGAN) FORSTER (1879–1970)

In *A Passage to India,* E. M. Forster depicts the irrecon-cilable psychological and cultural conflicts between indi-viduals, as well as between racial and religious groups, in 20th-century colonial India.

The central event in the novel concerns the alleged attempted rape in the Marabar Caves of an English-woman, Adela Quested, by a young Indian surgeon. The subsequent trial of Dr. Aziz does not reveal whether or not the attempted rape actually took place, nor is the truth disclosed by the book's plot.

Martin Seymour-Smith calls *A Passage to India* Forster's "finest achievement....He conveys a unique sense of the tragedy of the gap that lies between Indians and English-men...." Written years before the end of British rule in India, *A Passage to India* anticipates the troubled failure of England's colonial enterprise.

L'étranger (1942)

{The Stranger}

Albert Camus (1913–1960)

This novel's characteristic atmosphere stems from its author's early experiences as a poor child living in a vivid, primitive land of uncertain political status. Algeria in the 1930s was part province, part colony. Although it had been formally annexed by France in 1842, Arabs always outnumbered Europeans. Still, to most of its inhabitants, increased assimilation seemed inevitable. Certainly, few anticipated the violent nationalist uprising of 1954.

Albert Camus, raised by a stoical, illiterate mother in Belcourt, a teeming working-class quarter of Algiers, was singularly prescient. His biographer, Patrick McCarthy, writes, "Long before the Algerian War, he had depicted, however ambiguously, the murder of an Arab by a French Algerian. When that war broke out it plunged him into a depression that left him unable to write." Camus was awarded the Nobel Prize in Literature in 1957.

United Nations Charter (1945)

Thirteen days before the surrender of the Germans in World War II, on April 25, 1945, representatives of 46 nations convened in San Francisco, California. They were charged with drafting a document to structure the peace. The first major international conference in over 2,000 years that was not dominated by Europe, the meeting was attended by envoys from 21 Western Hemisphere republics, 7 Middle Eastern countries, 3 Soviet republics, 2 Far Eastern countries, and 2 African states, in addition to the Allies then fighting the war.

As the result of their labors, the United Nations came into official existence on October 24, 1945. Its purpose, as set out in the Charter, is to "save succeeding generations from the scourge of war...and to employ international machinery for the promotion of the economic and social advancement of all people...."

Cry, the Beloved Country (1948)*

ALAN PATON (1903–1988)

In his autobiography, Alan Paton observed that 1948 brought the "two decisive events" of his life, the publication of this best-selling book and the coming to power of the Afrikaner nationalists, "with their policies of rigid racial separation." In the novel, Paton lyrically describes the pilgrimage of Stephen Kumalo, an elderly Zulu minister, as he journeys through a land not yet scarred by the worst excesses of *apartheid*. Kumalo travels from his drought-stricken rural parish to Johannesburg, South Africa. In the suburb of Sophiatown, where blacks have freehold rights and some own houses and businesses, he looks for his lost son, Absalom.

In 1954, with little warning, the South African government obliterated Sophiatown and forcibly moved its 60,000 African inhabitants to a desolate encampment miles away. At first known only as the South Western Townships, this place later became known as Soweto.

The Family of Man: The Photographic Exhibition Created by Edward Steichen for the Museum of Modern Art (1955)

NEW YORK. MUSEUM OF MODERN ART
EDWARD STEICHEN (1879–1973)

When Edward Steichen was Director of the Department of Photography at the Museum of Modern Art, he organized what has been described as the greatest photographic exposition ever mounted. The 503 photographs from 68 countries that make up *The Family of Man* were exhibited from January 26 to May 8, 1955. Steichen's intention was to "mirror the essential oneness of mankind" by presenting images of all sorts of human activities: birth, work, play, life in and out of families, and death.

Reviewing the book on its publication in September of that year, *The New Yorker* described it as "at once pretentious, exasperating, and enormously captivating." The overall effect of the book's Whitmanesque lyricism remains stirring despite its sentimentality.

Things Fall Apart (1958)

CHINUA ACHEBE (b. 1930)

This is the story of Okonkwo, a prideful and hardworking Igbo farmer, who is destroyed by his conservative and righteous adherence to tribal customs even as they disintegrate around him.

Rural Nigeria in the late 19th century becomes intimate and familiar to readers of this novel. Daily life in Okonkwo's compound, the domestic routines of his wives, the play and anxieties of his children, all become known. Even such practices as the prescribed abandonment of twins at birth come to have a kind of inevitability.

Published in 1958, just two years before Nigeria gained political independence, this elegantly written, compassionate novel presents a view of West African life from within, not as interpreted by anthropologists, colonial administrators, or European writers of fiction.

Les damnés de la terre (1961)
[*The Wretched of the Earth*]

Frantz Fanon (1925–1961)

According to a review in *Time*, "this is not so much a book as a rock thrown through the windows of the West. It is the *Communist Manifesto* or the *Mein Kampf* of the anticolonial revolution...."

Fanon, born on the Caribbean island of Martinique, won the Croix de Guerre fighting with the Free French Forces during World War II, but by 1954 he was leading the opposition to the French army as a spokesperson for the FLN, the Algerian National Liberation Front. Also trained as a psychiatrist, he observed in patients the psychologically deforming effects of colonialism on both the occupiers and the colonized.

The theory of revolutionary nationalism promulgated in this book provided ideological underpinning for the American Black Power movement and influenced white student radicals of the 1960s.

Wide Sargasso Sea (1966)

JEAN RHYS (1890–1979)

To most readers, Bertha is a shadow of a character in Charlotte Brontë's *Jane Eyre*: the madwoman in the attic. To Jean Rhys, she was an invitation to re-imagine the story from its margins. *Wide Sargasso Sea* allows Antoinette—as Bertha is here called—to narrate her lush and lonely girlhood on the island of Jamaica. The slaves are newly freed, supernatural "obeah" confronts European wisdom and greed, and Rochester arrives from England determined to marry a rich white Creole. Caught between cultures, Antoinette pays for the colonial sins of her parents with her own violent displacement.

Rhys drew on her own West Indian childhood to give her heroine voice. Hailed for her early work and then rumored dead or mad, Rhys broke a 27-year silence to publish *Wide Sargasso Sea,* her fifth novel and her masterpiece.

Mawsim al-Hijra ila al-Shamal (1969)

{Season of Migration to the North}

TAYEB EL-SALIH (b. 1929)

In a lyrical voice, the narrator of *Season of Migration to the North* tells of his return to his native Sudanese village, where he encounters a stranger. The stranger's tale of a violent trip from Africa to England — and the narrator's own reactions — offer a haunting reversal of Joseph Conrad's great imperialist narrative, *Heart of Darkness*. At the same time, the story, with its blend of Western psychology, oral storytelling, and rejected romanticism, offers new directions to contemporary Arab literature.

Salih, born in Sudan and acclaimed throughout the Arab-speaking world, has been hailed for his efforts to link the Arabic, African, and Western traditions. This novel in particular "lies between the traditional categories of East and West," according to Saree Makdisi. Salih's earlier works include *The Wedding of Zein and Other Stories,* which has also been widely translated.

Guerrillas (1975)

V. S. NAIPAUL (b. 1932)

Writing in *The New York Times,* Jane Kramer called V. S. Naipaul "our scourge for truth, a Solzhenitsyn of the third world." In *Guerrillas,* a dark, complex novel exhibiting his lifelong themes of exile and marginality, Naipaul portrays a nameless Caribbean island where the landscape is scarred by abandoned industrial parks and the air is polluted by bauxite dust and smoke from small fires. Its diverse inhabitants are frightened of one another, but expend little energy seeking common ground. At Thrushcross Grange, a half-built, all-male, agricultural commune stagnating in the bush, Jimmy Ahmed (born Leung) simulates the role of charismatic revolutionary leader. The novel's violent events turn on his relationship with a rootless white couple, in the words of Paul Theroux, like "a series of shocks...a shroud slowly unwound from a bloody corpse."

The winner of many literary prizes, Naipaul was awarded a knighthood by Queen Elizabeth II in 1990.

The Bride Price (1976)

BUCHI EMECHETA (b. 1944)

Giving voice to the doubly colonized women of West Africa, Buchi Emecheta has produced several stunning novels; this one brings documentary realism to "a tale as sharp as a folk ballad."

Women in Emecheta's novels share the experience of being a kind of property. They are never quickly emancipated by exposure to Western values, in part because their men cling tenaciously to the one piece of traditional authority left to them: sovereignty within the family. In *The Bride Price,* a terrible retribution falls upon Aku-nna, an intelligent, gentle girl who elopes with a low-caste schoolmaster. Her stepfather's refusal to accept the customary Igbo wedding payment seals her doom.

Although rooted in the particular experience of Nigerian women, Emecheta's writing has universal application for women living in rapidly modernizing cultures throughout the world.

Cesarz (1978)

{The Emperor}

Ryszard Kapuściński (b. 1932)

The *Emperor* depicts the last days of the court of Haile Selassie of Ethiopia through a series of interviews with the members of the imperial court. For readers, however, the book transcends time and place to become a masterful study on the corruptive nature of power. In the author's native Poland, the book's Ethiopia became a metaphor for the Communist regime of the time.

The publication in English of *The Emperor* placed Kapuściński in the forefront of the New Journalism, alongside such acclaimed writers as Norman Mailer, Truman Capote, and Bruce Chatwin.

In a March 1993 *Vanity Fair* article about Kapuściński, Salman Rushdie noted: "When I first discovered *The Emperor*...it was quite clear from two pages that I was reading not just a reportage but a real work of art, a quite astounding piece of writing unlike anything I'd seen. I promptly became a kind of Kapuściński bore, where I would buttonhole people and force them to read this extraordinary book."

Me llamo Rigoberta Menchú y así me nació conciencia (1983)

{*I, Rigoberta Menchú*}

RIGOBERTA MENCHÚ (b. 1959)

After she was awarded the 1992 Nobel Peace Prize, Rigoberta Menchú received flowers at her home in exile, a communal residence in a poor quarter of Mexico City. According to *People* magazine, she also received anonymous messages warning that the bouquets were intended for her grave. Both the prize and the death threats resulted from Menchú's role in Guatemala's brutal civil conflict.

From her earliest years, Menchú worked as a peasant organizer among the Quiche, her own group, and other Indians. This book, testimonial rather than autobiography, was published to draw international attention to their cause. Assisted by Elizabeth Burgos-Debray, a Venezuelan ethnographer, Menchú tells about her childhood and about Quiche custom and ceremony. She also describes the murder of her parents, who were but two of over 150,000 victims of "internal colonialism," the genocidal war of oppression waged against indigenous peoples by the Guatemalan army in service to the land-owning class.

L'amant (1984)

{The Lover}

MARGUERITE DURAS (b. 1914)

Acclaimed for her 1959 screenplay, *Hiroshima mon amour,*
Marguerite Duras continues to explore in varied genres
the themes of desire, madness, and love set against a political backdrop. *The Lover* revisits a story of childhood passion first told by Duras in *The Sea Wall* (1950). Set near
Saigon, where Duras herself grew up, *The Lover* recounts
the affair between a wealthy Chinese man and the young
daughter of impoverished French colonists. Interracial
desire and hatred torment the lovers and their families,
while colonial tension and isolation lead to madness.

While critics unite in praising the work's structure —
its bold jumps in time and perspective, presented in flash-
ing images — they debate *The Lover*'s status as autobiography, colonial parable, or novel. It is in the last category
that *The Lover* won France's prestigious Prix Goncourt.

MIND & SPIRIT

F rom one vantage, the 20th century is the age of industry, of technology, of machines. But look again. In the last 100 years, human nature underwent as radical a remapping as did the universe. Freud opened new realms with the word "unconscious." Bettelheim reaffirmed fantasy, and William James the power of faith in a rational world. Many feared that religion would be replaced by science — or by psychedelic drugs, following Timothy Leary. But the oldest of teachings kept pace, as the Bible was translated anew. The human body was celebrated no

less than the spirit. Dr. Spock rethought the early years of life, and Dr. Kübler-Ross the end, while Havelock Ellis broached the topic of sex in the middle. These new visions of human nature also had a dark side. The individual mind could follow freedom to madness, as in Kesey's novels. Philosophy could lead to despair, following Sartre, and society to suicide (after Durkheim). But at the century's end, the life of the spirit thrives, alongside psychology, sociology, and other revolutionary human sciences.

Le suicide: étude de sociologie (1897)

{Suicide: A Study in Sociology}

EMILE DURKHEIM (1858–1917)

If most rational minds turn away from suicide, French sociologist Emile Durkheim looked more closely. Why was it, he wondered, that in each society a consistent number of people commit suicide each year? Following an ambitious statistical analysis, Durkheim outlined a theory. Suicide is less an aberration of the individual, he speculated, than it is a result of social causes. Durkheim detailed four causes in particular: egoism, altruism, anomie, and fatalism. With his study, Durkheim provided a language and a framework for discussing society as a whole, distinct from its individual members. The impulse toward suicide might begin with the individual, but in Durkheim's vision societies were more or less able to regulate those *courants suicidogènes* at any given moment. Modern society, with its weakening social and religious regulation, saw corresponding increases in the suicide rate. Although terms have changed, Durkheim's work remains a founding classic of sociology.

Die Traumdeutung (1900)

{The Interpretation of Dreams}

SIGMUND FREUD (1856–1939)

> *The Interpretation of Dreams* is the royal road to a knowledge
> of the unconscious activities of the brain.

The *Interpretation of Dreams* was actually published in
1899, but the title page was postdated into the new century that Freud's theories were to color so strongly. It was
in this work that Freud first elaborated his theory of psychoanalysis, surveying dream interpretation, the Oedipus
Complex, repression, and wish fulfillment. It is generally
considered to be Freud's most important work, drawing
upon his own self-analysis as well as the clinical work con-
ducted with his upper-class Viennese patients. By working to uncover the various motivations and desires behind
conscious mental functioning, Freud changed the way
people perceived not only themselves, but also the world
around them.

Studies in the Psychology of Sex (1901–28)

HAVELOCK ELLIS (1859–1939)

The sexual attitudes and theories of the 20th century have their roots in the rejection of 19th-century Victorian moral codes. Havelock Ellis was a pioneer in breaking through many of these sexual taboos. *Studies in the Psychology of Sex* not only brought together and classified various human sexual activities, it also challenged existing attitudes toward these behaviors. Using arguments drawn from both animal behavior and cultural relativism, Ellis sought to broaden the range of acceptable human sexual behavior. He is seen now as the first modern sexual theorist, and his work as a forerunner to that of Alfred Kinsey and Masters and Johnson.

The Varieties of Religious Experience: A Study in Human Nature (1902)

WILLIAM JAMES (1842–1910)

One of the most creative thinkers — and most lucid writers — of his day, William James helped bring many disciplines into the 20th century. He developed the first American school of philosophy, Pragmatism. He grounded the young field of psychology in experimental inquiry. He changed how we think about thought, coining the term "stream of consciousness" (and thus spurring modernist literature). Across all his endeavors, James respected life as it is *experienced,* not as it is theorized. This approach informs *The Varieties of Religious Experience.* If people experience religious ecstasy, he wrote, it must be real. Although we cannot rationally locate its source, it is possible to affirm the effects of faith. From case studies of many religions, James concluded that "we can experience union with *something* larger than ourselves and in that union find our greatest peace." A philosopher affirming values beyond rational inquiry, James lent a human face to a technological age.

The Prophet (1923)

KAHLIL GIBRAN (1883–1931)

Although born in Lebanon, Gibran had lived in the West and adopted English as his literary language by his early 20s. A prolific author, he is known primarily for one book, *The Prophet,* published in 1923 with his own illustrations. The prose poems that constitute most of the book are infused with a mystical and spiritual outlook encompassing love, freedom, good and evil, religion, and death.

The initial reaction to the book was modest, but by the 1960s it had become a cult classic. By the early 1970s, *The Prophet* had sold over four million copies and been translated into more than 20 languages. Its universal appeal has made it a popular source and inspiration for alternative readings in contemporary wedding ceremonies.

Why I Am Not a Christian (1927)

BERTRAND RUSSELL (1872–1970)

> One is often told that it is a very wrong thing to attack
> religion, because religion makes men virtuous. So I am
> told; I have not noticed it.

So said philosopher and mathematician Bertrand Russell, in typically astringent fashion, in "Why I Am Not a Christian," a lecture delivered in London on a Sunday in 1927. An eloquent articulation of the secularist viewpoint, "Why I Am Not a Christian" locates the basis of religion in "fear...fear of the mysterious, fear of defeat, fear of death." Russell's plainspoken hostility to all dogma, his insistence on logic and evidence, and his defense of mental freedom have made him a courageous and singular, if sometimes controversial, figure in modern culture.

When, in 1950, Russell received the Nobel Prize in Literature, the award citation praised him as "one of our time's brilliant spokesmen of rationality...a fearless champion of free speech and free thought in the West."

Coming of Age in Samoa (1928)

MARGARET MEAD (1901–1978)

In the midst of the ongoing "nature versus nurture" conflict of the post–World War I era, Margaret Mead caused
a sensation with the publication of *Coming of Age in Samoa,*
a product of her nine months of field work among the
natives of American Samoa. Siding firmly with anthropologist Franz Boas, her mentor at Columbia University,
Mead concluded that culture, not genetics, was the crucial
factor in determining human behavior and personality.
Although Mead has been criticized for subjectiveness and
inaccuracies in her work, the book still remains a classic,
and Margaret Mead is regarded as a pioneer in the field of
cultural anthropology.

L'être et le néant (1943)
{Being and Nothingness}

JEAN-PAUL SARTRE (1905–1980)

> L'homme est une passion inutile. ("Man is a useless passion.")

Arguably the most influential philosophical treatise written in this century, Jean-Paul Sartre's formidable work, a synthesis of his basic themes, was published in 1943, just as he was emerging as the leading light of Left Bank intellectual life. When the English translation appeared in 1956, Robert Peel, writing in the *Christian Science Monitor,* noted, "It exists as a powerful challenge to all optimistic abstractions that are not rooted in the concrete process of living."

Of course, the audience for technical philosophy is always limited, and Sartre's great popular reputation rests in part on his other writings, most notably his autobiography, *Les mots (The Words)* (1963), and his plays, especially *Les mouches (The Flies)* (1943). In 1964, Sartre was awarded the Nobel Prize in Literature, but declined to accept it.

The Common Sense Book of Baby and Child Care (1946)

(Dr.) Benjamin (McLane) Spock (b. 1903)

When it appeared in 1946, the advice in Dr. Spock's now classic book was a dramatic break from the prevailing "expert" opinion. Rather than force a baby into a strict behavioral schedule, Spock, who had training in both pediatrics and psychiatry, encouraged parents to use their own judgment and common sense.

Two factors helped make this book the "bible" it has become. First, it was published at the start of the baby boom, which provided a large audience of receptive new parents. Moreover, its publication coincided with the start of the paperback revolution, which made possible a low price and wide distribution. Pocket Books commissioned Dr. Spock to write the book, but arranged to have it first brought out as a hardcover by Duell, Sloan and Pearce, under the title *The Common Sense Book of Baby and Child Care* — to assure that it would be taken seriously by reviewers. Later the same year, *The Pocket Book of Baby and Child Care* appeared in paperback.

The Holy Bible. Revised Standard Version (1952)

By the middle of this century, scholarly investigation of ancient languages and biblical cultures had progressed sufficiently to warrant a comprehensive analysis and reworking of the King James Version of the Bible. The scholars responsible for this new translation sought to be true to the most ancient and reliable manuscripts while remaining sensitive to the rhythm and style of the King James Version. They understood their task to be to revise the latter, in light of contemporary scholarship, not to undertake a totally new translation from the original Greek and Hebrew texts.

The skill of the revisers in achieving their goal is reflected in the widespread use of the Revised Standard Version by Protestant churches in their worship services. In the ecumenical spirit of the 1960s, a special edition of the Revised Standard Version, adapted to Roman Catholic needs, was authorized by that Church for its lectionary.

The Courage to Be (1952)

Paul Tillich (1886–1965)

In his many books, the great Protestant theologian Paul Tillich addressed modern intellectual movements such as Marxism, psychoanalysis, and existentialism. After his dismissal from the University of Frankfurt for opposition to the Nazis, Tillich in 1933 came to teach at the Union Theological Seminary in New York. He later told a reporter for the *New York Post,* "I had the great honor and luck to be about the first non-Jewish professor dismissed from a German University."

Called by Rollo May "the most existential book written in America," *The Courage to Be* offered as its core message that "courage was essential to the experience of meaning of life. It was not merely one virtue among others, but the fundamental virtue upon which all others depend."

One Flew Over the Cuckoo's Nest (1962)

KEN KESEY (b. 1935)

Ken Kesey's first novel remains his most popular and enduring. In a mental hospital, the iconoclastic anti-hero, Randall Patrick McMurphy, is pitted against Nurse Ratched, who seeks to dominate, control, and bring into conformity the inmates under her jurisdiction. Although criticized for misogynistic and racist overtones, *One Flew Over the Cuckoo's Nest* still resonates with the classic theme of the individual rebelling against the controlling forces of society, and brings to mind Thomas Szaz's assertion that in the 20th century, "mental illness" is the label we pin on anyone who acts outside the accepted boundaries of behavior.

The Politics of Ecstasy (1968)

TIMOTHY LEARY (b. 1920)

The 1960s provided Timothy Leary, a teacher at Harvard, with an intellectual and cultural setting congenial to his unconventional ideas and activities. He was in many ways both the leader and most avid disciple of the many experimental practices and trends that were to characterize the decade.

In the essays that make up *The Politics of Ecstasy*, Leary promotes the use of psychedelic drugs such as LSD as a means to connect to an inner self and to attain a higher level of consciousness. LSD is recommended also as a means to enhance religious experience.

Although American society has rejected Leary's ideas about the positive nature of drugs, it has nevertheless benefited from his emphasis on individual aspirations, needs, and feelings and from the recognition that personal judgments, even those that conflict with societal norms, may have validity and worth.

Death and Dying (1969)

ELISABETH KÜBLER-ROSS (b. 1926)

Elisabeth Kübler-Ross's work as a psychiatrist with the terminally ill resulted in the publication of *On Death and Dying,* which challenged many 20th-century taboos and attitudes associated with death. Reacting to the isolation and sanitization of death she encountered in the hospitals she worked in, Kübler-Ross sought to make the medical establishment, and society, pay attention to the physical and psychological needs of the dying. Her work has resulted in the spread of the hospice movement in America, and in a more dignified and humane approach to the end of life.

The Uses of Enchantment (1976)

Bruno Bettelheim (1903–1990)

> . . . fairy tales, like all true works of art, possess a multifarious richness and depth that far transcend what even the most thorough discursive examination can reveal from them.

Although known primarily for his controversial work as a psychoanalyst with emotionally disturbed and autistic children, Bettelheim was also interested in the moral and psychological development of normal children. Fairy tales, in his view, allow children to make sense of a bewildering array of problems and feelings. Just as Freud contended that psychoanalysis allows adults to accept the problematic nature of life without being defeated by it, so, too, Bettelheim believed that the fairy tale helps children develop the resources to cope with and master the emotional hardships they encounter on the road to maturity. Today, the myths and fairy tales of various cultures are seen to offer ways of understanding all human behavior.

POPULAR CULTURE &
MASS ENTERTAINMENT

Sleuthing and terrorizing, satirizing and swooning, the heroes and heroines of this century's most popular literature kept pace with new competition, from Hollywood and television. Indeed, the literature of mass entertainment roamed more genres than either newcomer, and fueled the best ideas of both. Westerns go back to the galloping best-sellers of Zane Grey. Modern science fiction owes extraplanetary debt to Robert Heinlein. Agatha Christie "done it" for mysteries; Grace Metalious "bared all" in her

mini-saga *Peyton Place.* And who can shake the horror of Bram Stoker and Stephen King? Their visions still haunt Hollywood, which also borrowed *Gone with the Wind, The Big Sleep,* and *Tarzan of the Apes.* Still, some books could *only* be books. Dale Carnegie ushered in the age of self-help. Dr. Seuss made early reading fun. While Nathanael West's vision of a Hollywood in flames may carry the competition too far, it's fair to say that people still read for fun — before or even after they head out to see the movie version.

Dracula (1897)

BRAM STOKER (1847–1912)

Dracula appeared at a time when the public was fascinated by vampires. An immediate success, it was considered so terrifying that critics recommended hiding it from
children and nervous adults. It has subsequently been
hailed as the ultimate vampire novel, the most successful
horror novel in the English language, and even a masterpiece.

Anthony Boucher attributes this success to Bram
Stoker's innovative use of "contemporary naturalism."
Stoker made his horror lively, setting the action in 1893
London and referring to such modern scientific inventions
as the phonograph and Kodak photographs.

Although destroyed in the novel, the character of
Dracula has lived on in numerous stage and screen incarnations, TV movies, and a TV series. In addition, Dracula
has been the subject of numerous essays in the fields of
psychology, folklore, sociology, and popular culture. The
novel has never been out of print.

The Turn of the Screw (1898)

HENRY JAMES (1843–1916)

Oscar Wilde described Henry James's *The Turn of the Screw* as a "most wonderful, lurid, poisonous little tale." Few readers would disagree. It is a ghostly shocker that James himself termed a "pot-boiler."

Opening with a classic Christmas-tales-around-the-fire setting, James echoes the work of Charlotte Brontë in this ambiguous narration by an unnamed governess who is put in charge of two children at a lonely and sinister country estate. Intelligent and acutely perceptive, the heroine does battle with two libidinous ghosts who, appearing—horribly—only to her, have come to claim her charges.

The Turn of the Screw has elicited an enormous variety of critical responses. Is the haunting genuine? Is the governess a sexually repressed hysteric? The tale's enduring mystery and appeal are demonstrated by its many adaptations for stage and film, and especially by Benjamin Britten's opera, first produced in 1954.

The Hound of the Baskervilles (1902)

ARTHUR CONAN DOYLE (1859–1930)

Sherlock Holmes, the world's first consulting detective, is one of the most famous literary creations of all time, and *The Hound of the Baskervilles* is among the most popular of all the tales starring Holmes and his partner, Doctor Watson. One reason for its popularity was that the novel, set in 1889, was written and published after Conan Doyle had "killed off" Holmes in 1894 in "The Final Problem," much to the dismay of readers. (It wasn't until 1905 that Conan Doyle officially resurrected his hero in "The Return of Sherlock Holmes.") This full-length novel is considered one of Conan Doyle's most literary and best-written works. In it he skillfully pits Holmes at his deductive best against the ghostly landscape of the Dartmouth moors.

The characters of Holmes and Watson have acquired international fame and appear regularly in numerous reprints, parodies, and pastiches as well as comic strips, comic books, movies, and TV series.

Tarzan of the Apes (1912)

EDGAR RICE BURROUGHS (1875–1950)

Tarzan of the Apes was serialized in *All-Story Magazine* in 1912, and published separately in 1914. The world watched in wonder as an orphaned English nobleman raised by African apes discovered his human heritage, and taught himself to become "Lord of the jungle." The popularity of Tarzan spurred Burroughs to produce 23 sequels. Tarzan has since become one of the world's most popular fictional characters, appearing in numerous movies, TV series, newspaper comic strips, and comic books.

Ray Bradbury recalled the magic of Tarzan: "Mr. Burroughs convinced me that I could talk with the animals, even if they didn't answer back, and that late nights when I was asleep my soul slipped from my body, slung itself out the window, and frolicked across town never touching the lawns, always hanging from trees where, even later in those nights, I taught myself alphabets and soon learned French and English and danced with the apes when the moon rose."

Riders of the Purple Sage (1912)

ZANE GREY (1872–1939)

Zane Grey, the "Father of the Western," produced more than 50 novels, the most significant of which is *Riders of the Purple Sage*. The first Western ever to hit the best-seller lists, it is an enduring favorite. This adventure romance, set in southern Utah, brewed up the formula that has been followed by every successful Western since. Lassiter, the rough and ready "cowboy gunman" hero, and Jane Withersteen, the strong, independent heroine, meet dastardly villains and contend with gunfights, cattle stampedes, and avalanches.

Critics praised Grey for his vivid portrayals of the American West, brimming with colorful and sympathetic characters. In Grey's hands, the 19th-century dime novel Western became a respectable 20th-century literary genre.

Many of Grey's novels have been adapted as films starring such notables as John Wayne, Roy Rogers, and Randolph Scott. Currently, over 10 million copies of Grey's novels are in print.

The Mysterious Affair at Styles (1920)

AGATHA CHRISTIE (1890–1976)

The Mysterious Affair at Styles introduced the world to two lasting heroes: new author Agatha Christie, and her sleuthing protagonist, Hercule Poirot. Poirot was recognizably descended from such other memorable detectives as Auguste Dupin and Sherlock Holmes, sharing their methodical and astute attention to detail. But he had a modern bent, and a knack for cracking the country-house intrigues Christie developed to a tee. One by one, each character from a limited and quirky cast would come under suspicion. Christie's newfangled mysteries appealed to the current vogue for the enjoyment of murder as the opportunity for solving a puzzle.

Beginning with this book, her plots were lifted above their mechanical regularity by the entertaining idiosyncracies of Poirot himself. Christie ushered in the "Golden Age" of crime novels, and continues to mystify — and delight — her many faithful readers.

How to Win Friends and Influence People (1936)

DALE CARNEGIE (1888–1955)

Dale Carnegie's famous public speaking course had been in existence for 24 years before he published it in book form in 1936 in the midst of the Depression. The book was scorned by academics and considered complacent by social reformers, but it went on to become a perennial best-seller, eternally in print and the vanguard of the vast self-help psychology publishing movement.

Carnegie's goal was to bring optimism to the life of the average working person. He taught that human relations skills were the key to success, and that such skills — getting along with people and getting things done — could be acquired. He believed that his course could have profound personal and societal impact. Financial success was one form of compensation, but Carnegie also promised increased self-confidence, contentment, and more pleasure out of life. Cultural historians see Carnegie's work as one sign of the shift from an "Age of Character" to an "Age of Personality," in which new skills were needed to negotiate what David Riesman called "the lonely crowd."

Gone with the Wind (1936)

MARGARET MITCHELL (1900–1949)

Margaret Mitchell's sweeping rendition of a South torn apart by civil war — of Scarlett O'Hara fighting for herself, Rhett, and Tara; of soldiers marching; of Atlanta burning — has become national mythology. When Hollywood captured Mitchell's vision on film three years later, some of the dialogue entered the vernacular. Behind the mythology lies a historical romance written by one southern woman, who drew upon childhood stories and meticulous research to recreate a lost world. Today, *Gone with the Wind* remains the best-selling American novel ever, selling more hardcover copies than any other book save the Bible.

Critics have pondered the book's mass appeal, crediting its fiery heroine, its tribute to a paradise lost, its "subpornographic" eroticism, and the comfort it offered to mid-Depression America. While some have scorned the book's "stylelessness," others have praised it for its fantastic scope — including the Pulitzer Prize committee, which bypassed Dos Passos, Faulkner, and Santayana to honor Mitchell in 1937.

The Big Sleep (1939)

RAYMOND CHANDLER (1888–1959)

> Down these mean streets a man must go who is not him-
> self mean, who is neither tarnished nor afraid....He is the
> hero; he is everything. He must be a complete man and
> a common man and yet an unusual man.

This is the Code of the Private Eye as defined by Raymond Chandler in his 1944 essay "The Simple Act of
Murder." Such a man was Philip Marlowe, private eye, an
educated, heroic, streetwise, rugged individualist and the
hero of Chandler's first novel, *The Big Sleep*. This work
established Chandler as the master of the "hard-boiled"
detective novel, and his articulate and literary style of
writing won him a large audience, which ranged from the
man in the street to the most sophisticated intellectual.
Marlowe subsequently appeared in a series of extremely
popular novels, among them *The Lady in the Lake, The
Long Goodbye,* and *Farewell, My Lovely.* His character was
also portrayed in movies and a TV series.

The Day of the Locust (1939)

NATHANAEL WEST (1913–1940)

Described in reviews of the time as "surrealistic," *The Day of the Locust* seems less so as time passes. West's themes—disillusionment and cynicism, physical violence as a result of spiritual malaise—are still with us. A forerunner of later black humorists and fantasists, West used joyless, derisive humor to unmask the illusions that destroy people's lives. West's admirers included F. Scott Fitzgerald, and his work has steadily gained in popularity. In another novel, *Miss Lonelyhearts,* he created a cultural prototype with the bittersweet hero, a newspaperman who tries to save the world through his advice-to-the-lovelorn column.

In an early review of the apocalyptic *Day of the Locust,* Clifton Fadiman proclaimed it a "book about Hollywood that has all the fascination of a nice bit of phosphorescent decay...an unpleasant, thoroughly original book."

Peyton Place (1956)

GRACE METALIOUS (1924–1964)

Rape, murder, suicide, incest, abortion, seduction, and drunken binges are among the lurid activities in this saga for a new reading sensibility. The modern literary soap opera (with heart) began here, as readers followed ten years in the life of a small New England town as Alison MacKenzie, illegitimate child of the respectable neighborhood, and Selena Cross, her abused best friend from the wrong side of the tracks, grow from adolescence to maturity.

The New York Times Book Review called the book a "Small Town Peep Show," adding: "The late Sinclair Lewis would no doubt have hailed Grace Metalious as a sister-in-arms against the false fronts and bourgeois pretentions of allegedly respectable communities, and certified her as a public accountant of what goes on in the basements, bedrooms and back porches of a 'typical American town.'"

The Cat in the Hat (1957)

DR. (THEODOR) SEUSS (GEISEL)
(1904–1991)

From babies to grown-ups and all in between,
Who can't remember Sam's Ham and Eggs Green?
The Lorax! and Horton!
And Star-bellied Sneetches!
Dr. Seuss brought new readers
To jubilant reaches.
Oh — "Thing One" and "Thing Two,"
And *If I Ran the Zoo,*
But more loved than that
Was *The Cat in the Hat.*
It sold by the millions!
It thrilled all the chillions
Who'd grown bored with old Dick, Jane and Spot.
It started a trend
That will thrill to the end:
That's *reading* for color and plot!

— NINA SONENBERG

Stranger in a Strange Land (1961)

ROBERT A. HEINLEIN (1907–1988)

Robert A. Heinlein, a "Grand Master" of 20th-century science fiction, wrote numerous award-winning short stories and novels. The most famous and influential of his novels, the Hugo Award-winning *Stranger in a Strange Land,* is the story of Valentine Michael Smith, a human raised on Mars by Martians. Back on Earth, Valentine displays unusual extrasensory powers and becomes the focus of a cult following. Throughout the novel, Heinlein takes deadly critical aim at practically every cultural norm of American society. Among the many controversial subjects touched upon are "free love," cannibalism, iconoclasm, and the use of recreational drugs. Certain phrases made their way into the vocabulary of 1960s "flower children": "grokking to fullness," "waiting is," and "thou art God." The book was the first SF novel to make the bestseller lists and to earn a cult following on college campuses.

Catch-22 (1961)

Joseph Heller (b. 1923)

Catch-22, Joseph Heller's first and best-known novel, depicts a military world turned upside down. In Heller's World War II, a supplies manager has more power than a general, and anyone seeking a discharge on the grounds of insanity is declared sane enough to keep on fighting.

When the novel appeared in 1961, World War II veterans appreciated its satire of the military bureaucracy and the chaos of war. By the mid-1960s, it had become a cult classic among counterculture activists for its biting indictment of war.

Catch-22 has since inspired a one-act play and a motion picture (1970). Many consider the novel to be the definitive statement of the modern antiwar position. The phrase "Catch-22," symbolizing the absurdity of all institutional logic, has become a permanent part of our language.

In 1994, Heller published *Closing Time: The Sequel to Catch-22*.

In Cold Blood: A True Account of a Multiple Murder and Its Consequences (1965)

TRUMAN CAPOTE (1924–1984)

On November 15, 1959, a Kansas couple and their two teenaged children were bound, gagged, and murdered in their beds. Even before suspects were identified, Truman Capote moved to Holcomb, Kansas, and began asking questions. Six years later, after the guilty were hanged, Capote published *In Cold Blood.* He declared his work the first in a new genre: the "nonfiction novel."

Hugely popular, the book met with varied critical response. *The New York Times* hailed Capote's blending of research, psychology, and novelistic re-creation as "a masterpiece — agonizing, terrible, possessed." Many questioned its status — was it documentary? Was it social protest? (Capote strongly opposed the death penalty.) Was it a moral offense? (Should real-world murder entertain?) Was it literature? Although less gruesome than books and films that followed, Capote's work established techniques of true-crime reportage that continue to haunt as they capture the tragedies of our times.

Ball Four: My Life and Hard Times Throwing the Knuckleball in the Big Leagues (1970)

Jim Bouton (b. 1939)

Jim Bouton's diaristic insider's account of the 1969 baseball season, during which he was a marginal relief pitcher for the Seattle Pilots and Houston Astros, remains one of the all-time best-selling sports books. Considered frank and irreverent, even scandalous, in 1970, it immediately drew the censure of the baseball establishment.

Ball Four was the first ripple of a tidal wave of "tell-all" books that have become commonplace not only in sports, but also in politics, entertainment, and other realms of contemporary public life.

Of great interest today, in light of the 1994–95 baseball strike, are the references to the bitterness and rancor that characterize owner-player relations, and to the early efforts of Marvin Miller to organize a players' union.

Carrie (1974)

STEPHEN KING (b. 1947)

An introverted teenaged girl, harassed by her Bible-thumping mother and her peers, discovers she has telekinetic powers and uses them to exact a terrifying revenge on her tormentors. *Carrie* immediately hit the best-seller lists, and the 1975 paperback edition sold over a million copies. The book was subsequently turned into a movie that made Sissy Spacek a star. Thus began the career of Stephen King, the most successful best-seller novelist in history.

Critics have attributed King's phenomenal success to his talent for placing ordinary people in contemporary American, often small-town Maine, settings and seamlessly weaving them into fantastic situations. The impossible becomes believable.

Since 1974, King's books have sold over 100 million copies. Many of his novels and novellas have been adapted into movies, such as *The Shining, Stand by Me,* and *The Shawshank Redemption,* and the television miniseries *The Stand.*

The Bonfire of the Vanities (1987)

TOM WOLFE (b. 1931)

Described by Jonathan Yardley as "a superb human comedy and the first novel ever to get contemporary New York, in all its arrogance and shame and heterogeneity and insularity, exactly right," this popular novel details the downfall of the arrogant and wealthy Sherman McCoy. McCoy, a self-declared "Master of the Universe," meets legal trouble — and more — when the car his mistress is driving injures a young black man in the Bronx. Nicholas Lemann asserts that "Wolfe's New York is pretty much the hellish place imagined by people who don't live there," adding, "there are echoes throughout of the classic American twentieth-century novels about the snatching away of worldly success, such as *An American Tragedy....* The allusion to the towering classic of this genre, *The Great Gatsby,* is direct and unmistakable." Wolfe himself has described the novel as a social critique of the realistic type the modern world needs most.

WOMEN RISE

One hundred years ago, American women could not vote. Their writing was often circumspect, typically avoiding both sex and politics. African American women writers knew their stories would be edited to suit a white readership. Still, even in the genteelest of fictions, tensions peeked through. Edith Wharton recreated the aristocratic past, and saw dissent in hushed tones. Continuing a struggle begun before the Civil War, women of the early 20th century took to soapboxes. They demanded the vote (and Carrie Chapman Catt wrote about their triumph). They demanded birth control (and Margaret

Sanger wrote about her fight). Tremendous gains were followed by mid-century silence. And then a jolt arrived from France; Simone de Beauvoir told women how men saw them, and called for sweeping change. American women of the 1960s climbed back atop soapboxes, aided by television, community meetings, and impassioned life stories. Maya Angelou told her story, finding a distinctive African American voice. Alice Walker and Susan Brownmiller discussed rape — and made it political. Modern women don't fear asking questions. Unfortunately, they don't always like the answers.

The Age of Innocence (1920)

EDITH WHARTON (1862–1937)

The year American women finally won suffrage, Edith Wharton published her Pulitzer Prize – winning novel, *The Age of Innocence.* At once a look back and a look forward, the novel pitted the respectable May Welland, seemingly passive and confined, against the outspoken Countess Ellen Olenska, newly returned from a bad marriage in Europe. The competition between the two women — and their world views — unfolds against a sweeping rendition of New York society, set in a romanticized, prewar past. Wharton both satirized and enshrined the aristocratic society she herself had inhabited, and recorded the rumblings that would bring its collapse. Writes Margaret McDowell: "It would be hard to find a book in which the problems of a group of people at a certain time are more carefully perceived, their manners and conventions more meticulously documented and criticized...and the conflicts between tradition and change more memorably dramatized."

Woman Suffrage and Politics: The Inner Story of the Suffrage Movement (1923)

CARRIE CHAPMAN CATT (1859–1947)

In this book, international activist Carrie Chapman Catt looked back on 72 years of grassroots struggle for women's suffrage in the United States. She recorded a ceaseless campaign on the state and federal levels, enlisting the energy and funds of thousands.

> When, during the last decade, the great suffrage parades...went marching through the streets of the cities and towns of America;...when the suffragist on the soap box was heard on every street corner; when huge suffrage mass meetings were packing auditoriums...; when suffrage was in everybody's mouth and on the front page of every newspaper, few paused to ask how it all started....It was just there, like breakfast.

Youthful America seemed the world's natural leader in this cause. Yet political interests delayed women's suffrage here for decades, as 26 other nations gave women the vote.

My Fight for Birth Control (1931)

MARGARET SANGER (1879–1966)

As a nurse-midwife on the Lower East Side of New York in the early years of this century, Margaret Sanger was sought after. As she noted in her autobiography:

> As soon as the neighbors learned that a nurse was in the building they came in…to visit, often carrying fruit, jellies, or gefüllter fish made after a cherished recipe. It was infinitely pathetic to me that they, so poor themselves, should bring me food. Later…was the question, "I am pregnant (or my daughter, or my sister is). Tell me something to keep from having another baby. We cannot afford another yet."

Margaret Sanger never forgot these women. Without money, advanced education, or influential friends, but with a belief that her cause was necessary and right, she spent her life leading the fight for birth control.

Dust Tracks on a Road (1942)

Zora Neale Hurston (1901–1960)

A decade after Zora Neale Hurston died in poverty, Alice Walker found the writer's unmarked gravesite. Raising a memorial stone to "A Genius of the South — Novelist, Folklorist, Anthropologist," Walker also rekindled literary interest in Hurston. *Dust Tracks on a Road,* although edited to please a white audience, tells Hurston's story in her own words.

Raised in Florida, in the first incorporated black town in America, young Zora had a mother who wouldn't "squinch her spirit." Taking herself North, Hurston attended Barnard and played a key role in the Harlem Renaissance. Langston Hughes described Hurston in *The Big Sea* as "full of side-splitting anecdotes, humorous tales, and tragicomic stories, remembered out of her life in the South." Hurston would go on to write her stories into the novels *Their Eyes Were Watching God* and *Jonah's Gourd Vine,* and to collect the folktales of others in *Mules and Men* — all acclaimed today.

Le deuxième sexe (1949)

{The Second Sex}

SIMONE DE BEAUVOIR (1908–1986)

Just when the world thought feminism dead, Simone de Beauvoir published her incendiary study, *Le deuxième sexe.* The first week, 22,000 copies were sold; the Vatican classed the book "forbidden." In hundreds of pages of lucidly argued philosophy, history, literary critique, and personal reflection, de Beauvoir demonstrated that men had relegated women to secondary status. If he was the essential "Subject, the Absolute," she was inessential, or "Other." What's more, wrote de Beauvoir, "One is not born, but rather becomes a woman." With these words, de Beauvoir opened a debate that still rages about the nature of femininity, and women's roles in society. Writes Ellen Willis: "Nearly four decades after it was first published in France, despite all the commentary the feminist movement has produced in the meantime, dated and parochial as it is in many respects, *The Second Sex* remains the most cogent and thorough book of feminist theory yet written."

The Golden Notebook (1962)

DORIS LESSING (b. 1919)

Anna Wulf, the heroine of Doris Lessing's landmark novel, comes close to breakdown in the course of *The Golden Notebook*. A complex and rebellious character, Anna has already written a successful novel, lived in Africa, joined the English Communist party, and undergone psychoanalysis. With increasing panic, she struggles to integrate the disparate parts of herself—each recorded in a different-colored notebook—into one all-embracing "golden notebook." The reader sees these notebooks, as well as Anna's outside world of politics, relationships, and close female friendships. Critics have read Anna as a part-fictional, part-autobiographical model of the path to "liberation" through self-scrutiny and political struggle. Writes Pearl Bell, "The book that established Doris Lessing as an influential feminist mentor, *The Golden Notebook*, was informed by aching honesty and a probing intelligence." Lessing has also written science fiction, journalism, travel essays, short stories, and drama.

The Feminine Mystique (1963)

BETTY FRIEDAN (b. 1921)

Betty Friedan's groundbreaking book was one of the first to articulate the malaise affecting white, middle-class, educated American women:

> The problem lay buried, unspoken, for many years in the minds of American women. It was a strange stirring, a sense of dissatisfaction....Each suburban wife struggled with it alone. As she made the beds, shopped for groceries, matched slipcover material, ate peanut butter sandwiches with her children, chauffeured Cub Scouts and Brownies, lay beside her husband at night—she was afraid to ask even of herself the silent question—"Is this all?"

Opening the question propelled Friedan to the front of America's feminist movement.

In her preface, Friedan acknowledges "the New York Public Library and its provision to a writer of quiet workspace and continuous access to research sources" — the exact prescription for feminine development set forth by Virginia Woolf in *A Room of One's Own.*

I Know Why the Caged Bird Sings (1969)

Maya Angelou (Marguerite Johnson) (b. 1928)

"Thou shall not be dirty" and "Thou shall not be impudent" were commandments of the author's childhood in segregated Stamps, Arkansas, a town visited regularly by the Ku Klux Klan. Raised in her grandmother's home, where hard work and church-going were emphasized, young Marguerite dreamed of waking from her "black ugly dream." Meanwhile, a town dentist refused to extract aching teeth: "My policy is I'd rather stick my hand in a dog's mouth than a nigger's."

Books became Angelou's escape until she moved to San Francisco to attend college. There she had a son at age 16, and became the first black woman streetcar conductor. *I Know Why the Caged Bird Sings* is the first volume of Angelou's four-part life history. Together, the books opened doors to truthful African American autobiography, and to greater understanding between races.

Maya Angelou was commissioned to commemorate President Bill Clinton's inauguration in poetry.

Sisterhood Is Powerful: An Anthology of Writings from the Women's Liberation Movement (1970)

ROBIN MORGAN (b. 1941), EDITOR

Sisterhood Is Powerful is testimony from the "second wave" of the American women's liberation movement; this collection "combines all sorts of articles, poems, graphics and sundry papers. These are the well-documented, statistically solid pieces and the intensely personal experiences . . . intended to reflect the wide spectrum of political theory and action that is women's liberation" (Introduction).

The energy, optimism, and idealism inherent in the movement of the 1970s is apparent in these pages. From the perspective of 26 years later, it is chilling to read Robin Morgan's caveat: "I fear for the women's movement's falling into precisely the same trap as did our foremothers, the suffragists; creating a bourgeois feminist movement that never quite dared enough, never questioned enough, never really reached out beyond its own class and race."

Against Our Will: Men, Women and Rape (1975)

Susan Brownmiller (b. 1935)

> Man's discovery that his genitalia could serve as a weapon to generate fear must rank as one of the most important discoveries of prehistoric times....It is nothing more or less than a conscious process of intimidation by which all men keep all women in a state of fear.

So declared Susan Brownmiller in her polemic history of rape as seen from a feminist perspective, touching on rape's use and meaning in wars throughout history. Brownmiller looked at homosexual rape, child molestation, and interracial rape. To round off her devastating analysis, she pulled in Freudian psychology, social and legal issues, and the "glamorization" of rape in popular culture.

Declaring that rape is not just a woman's problem, but a societal problem arising from "a distorted masculine philosophy of aggression," the author urges women to fight back, in their own way.

The Color Purple (1982)

ALICE WALKER (b. 1944)

The success of Alice Walker's third novel, *The Color Purple,* led to a movie deal, a Pulitzer Prize, and controversy. At the center is the distinctive voice of Celie. Like Walker, Celie grew up poor and black in the American South. With no one else to confide in, Celie begins a series of letters to God. These letters—and later ones addressed to a rediscovered sister who is living in Africa — track Celie's progress from rape and self-hatred, to a bad marriage, to love and self-discovery with another woman. Celie thus captures the struggle of downtrodden women for autonomy and spiritual wholeness. Critics have both praised and attacked Walker's use of black folk English to capture Celie's perspective. Walker responded: "Language is an intrinsic part of who we are and what has, for good or evil, happened to us. And, amazingly, it has sustained us more securely than the arms of angels."

Economics & Technology

You may never have cuddled up with a book on economics or technology. So you might be surprised to learn how thoroughly books in these fields have considered — and affected — your daily life. How do you decide what to wear in the morning? Thorstein Veblen offers a few choice words to describe your efforts at self-presentation. Why even get up to go to work? Max Weber considered the question of himself, and founded a social science with his answer. Economists from Keynes to Friedman and

Galbraith revolutionized Western ideas about money and government, affecting each dollar you earn and spend. Their sweeping visions grounded the industrial age, and helped launch the post-industrial one. Even when visionaries thought small — as Jacobs explored city neighborhoods; Schumacher villages; Henry Adams himself— they had an eye to a future being shaped by technology. All helped lead us to the Internet's gateway, where we look to new technological visionaries to put possibilities online.

The Theory of the Leisure Class: An Economic Study of Institutions (1899)

THORSTEIN (BUNDE) VEBLEN (1857–1929)

The words of Thorstein Veblen have become so familiar that it is easy to forget how pompous and outrageous they seemed in their day. With phrases like "conspicuous consumption" and "conspicuous waste," Veblen described and mocked the habits of the "leisure class" (itself a satiric label). Feigning objectivity, Veblen drew on economics, anthropology, and history to connect the acquisitive behavior of the modern gentleman with that of the Papuan chieftain. According to the author, each devotes his life not to productive "furtherance of human life," but rather to ensuring his own "good fame" through display of useless dress, goods, and knowledge.

Critics such as Alfred Kazin see "delightful irony" in Veblen's polysyllabic prose. Still, Veblen was devastating in his critique of American capitalist society. Writes John Kenneth Galbraith, "No one who has read this book ever again sees the consumption of goods in the same light."

Die protestantische Ethik und der Geist des Kapitalismus (1904)

{The Protestant Ethic and the Spirit of Capitalism}

Max Weber (1864–1920)

On the brink of collapse, German sociologist Max Weber began to contemplate his habits of compulsive labor. Five years later—after an extended illness—he undertook a vast new research project. Weber linked his own tireless work with his Calvinist upbringing, and soon found a correlation between all German capitalist ventures and a Protestant background. The theory Weber developed lives on in the term "Protestant work ethic," and helped found modern sociology. As Weber saw it, Calvinism was the first religion to view worldly riches as a sign of divine grace. The spread of Calvinism throughout Europe might therefore explain the sudden rise of capitalism.

Weber's work ranged across the social sciences and revolutionized methods of research. Keeping his focus on the role of ideas and of individual action within society, Weber pondered the move from the "light cloak" of worldly pursuit to the "iron cage" of modern bureaucracy.

The Education of Henry Adams (1907)

HENRY ADAMS (1838–1918)

Historian Henry Adams, a direct descendant of two American Presidents, published his *Education*...tentatively at first, in a private printing for a small group of friends. A public edition did not appear until 11 years later, in 1918. The book articulates a deeply troubling issue that still haunts industrialized societies: can spiritual and humane values, which Adams sees as legacies of the past, survive in a world dominated by technology?

Wrote Adams: "At the rate of progress since 1800, every American who lived into the year 2000 would know how to control unlimited power. He would think in complexities unimaginable to an earlier mind. He would deal with problems altogether beyond the range of earlier society. To him, the nineteenth century would stand on the same plane with the fourth—equally childlike—and he would only wonder how both of them, knowing so little, and so weak in force, should have done so much."

The General Theory of Employment, Interest and Money (1936)

John Maynard Keynes (1883–1946)

The most influential economist of the century, Keynes turned economic theory on its head. Before the English intellectual parted company with his peers, he too believed the economy self-correcting. But the theory didn't work — as evidenced by increasingly painful cycles of boom and bust throughout the West. In the middle of the Great Depression, Keynes published his landmark study urging the government to *spend* to spur recovery. Spending, predicted Keynes, would stimulate investment and create jobs. Shocked laissez-faire conservatives watched as Keynes's ideas guided America's New Deal and established the field of macroeconomics.

"Whether Keynes be seen as a conservative innovator seeking to strengthen the market economy or as a radical threat to the system, he has been *the* economist to be reckoned with," writes Warren Samuels. Following Keynes, many governments still control interest rates, spend during slow times, and view unemployment as a problem of the system, not the individual.

The Road to Serfdom (1944)[*]

FRIEDRICH A. VON HAYEK (1899–1992)

At a time when others were seeking an explanation for the horrors of Nazism in the moral inadequacies of the "German character," Friedrich A. von Hayek forcefully argued that socialism — indeed, any kind of centralized economic planning — leads to totalitarianism. Asserting that "Nazism is simply collectivism freed from all traces of an individualist tradition," he went on to define individualism as "an attitude of humility...and of tolerance to other opinions,...the exact opposite of the intellectual *hubris* which is at the root of the demand for comprehensive direction of social progress."

Hayek's immediate concern was that sudden, destabilizing unemployment after the war would lead Great Britain's leaders to institute socialist reforms. Although the postwar welfare state did not evolve into fascism, Hayek's theories retained their persuasiveness. He was awarded the Nobel Memorial Prize in Economics in 1974, and his ideas greatly influenced the free market policies of former Prime Minister Margaret Thatcher.

A Theory of the Consumption Function (1957)

MILTON FRIEDMAN (b. 1912)

How do consumers make decisions? How can government influence their actions or options — or should it at all? Milton Friedman offered conservative answers to the great questions of economics, at the same time challenging economic thought since Keynes. In this book, Friedman disputes Keynes's idea that aggregate spending and income are directly linked (and therefore open to government influence). Rather, he writes, consumers spend independent of government policy, based on their expected long-term, or "permanent," income. In all his writing, Friedman embraces a laissez-faire approach that celebrates individual freedom. He sees the ideal role for government as "umpire," not "parent."

Friedman's views influenced American and English politics in the 1970s and 1980s as these governments moved away from social service spending. The leader of the "monetarist" school, which emphasizes a stable money supply as one of government's few fiscal concerns, Friedman was awarded the Nobel Memorial Prize in Economics in 1976.

The Affluent Society (1958)

JOHN KENNETH GALBRAITH (b. 1908)

Few economics books have been hailed as "exciting," "exceptionally provocative," and "written with charm, wit, and bite." But Harvard economist John Kenneth Galbraith has earned fame both for the impact of his ideas and for his ability to communicate them to specialist and lay reader alike. The above comments greeted Galbraith's book *The Affluent Society,* which, for all its resemblance to a "page-turner," had a pressing message. Galbraith saw as perilous the modern economy's focus on ever-increasing production. Such a focus increased the violence of boom-bust cycles and inflation, Galbraith argued, and masked growing social imbalance.

Following Keynes, Galbraith urged public investment in social programs. But where Keynes saw this as a means to stimulate the economy's own forces of recovery, Galbraith hoped government would fund services that private interests alone would not support. Only through such social concern, wrote Galbraith, would society become mature, and not merely "affluent."

The Death and Life of Great American Cities (1961)

JANE JACOBS (b. 1916)

With this sardonic critique of mid-20th-century city planning, Jane Jacobs challenged the orthodoxy of development. She showed how massive urban-renewal and highway-building projects typically result in monotony and decay, while at the same time destroying the lively, diversified, and economically productive city neighborhoods they replace. Her analysis, which seems obvious today, was perceived in 1961 as an audacious attack on the consensus view of enlightened architects, politicians, and bankers.

Jacobs's affectionate descriptions of her own Greenwich Village neighborhood in the 1950s, and her discussion of the successful fight against a plan to build a bypass for truck traffic through Washington Square Park, make this book a favorite of many New Yorkers.

Superhighway — Super Hoax (1970)

Helen Leavitt (b. 1932)

> The Interstate Highway System is the largest single public works project ever undertaken by man.

In her impassioned polemic, Helen Leavitt reveals how a group she calls the "highwaymen," who include automobile manufacturers, oil company executives, members of the American Road Builders' Association, and government officials, worked in concert to promote the country's network of federally funded high-speed roadways. The book's argument and central paradox, that most superhighways bring increased traffic congestion rather than less, has never been effectively countered. Leavitt points out that other consequences of the construction of the Interstate System have also been harmful; most notably, she demonstrates environmental degradation, strangled cities, and ruined public transportation systems.

Small Is Beautiful: A Study of Economics as if People Mattered (1973)

E(RNST) F. SCHUMACHER (1911–1977)

Part economist and part spiritual leader, E. F. Schumacher earned a cult following with this widely read book. Trained in classical economics, the German-born reformist served as a longtime policy adviser to the British government. Becoming disillusioned with Western materialism, Schumacher began to link Christian and Buddhist tenets with thoughts on mankind's technological future. In *Small Is Beautiful,* he issued a call for "technology with a human face." Moralistic and impassioned, Schumacher won converts to ecological conservation, economic self-discipline, and respect for small communities and efforts throughout the world. "Man is small and, therefore, small is beautiful," he wrote. "To go for giantism is to go for self-destruction."

Critics bemoaned Schumacher's "astonishing absence of specificity" in his prescriptions for a modernized world. But his influence pervaded the counterculture and the "green" movement, and lasts in the belief that "appropriate technology" offers hope for the planet and its inhabitants.

The Whole Internet: User's Guide & Catalog (1992)

ED KROL (b. 1962)

Few phenomena in recent memory have captured the public's imagination as has the Internet, with its promise of virtual community and its role in the information revolution. Krol's published guide was one of the first to help tame this rich maze for ordinary computer users.

As a network manager at the National Center for Supercomputer Applications of the University of Illinois, Krol recognized the need for clear documentation for this amorphous and wildly growing network of networks. He wrote "Hitchhiker's Guide to the Internet" (available via file transfer on the network) "because he had so much trouble getting information and was sick of telling the same story to everyone." Then, with *The Whole Internet,* he reached out to a wide audience, writing not only with technical expertise, but also with enthusiasm for the subject and a genuine desire to open up to the curious the world of networking.

UTOPIAS & DYSTOPIAS

We all wonder what the future may bring. Flying machines, an independent Jewish state, test-tube babies, and feminists were all imagined by writers long before reality caught up. But some of these visions still elude us. Eternal youth remains the preserve of Sir James Barrie's *Peter Pan;* the hero of James Hilton's *Lost Horizon* was too human for "Shangri-La." In these visions, humanity persists in the face of technological marvels, such as Wells's time machine and Orwell's Big Brother. (Even Oz was run by a fragile wizard.) Of course, sometimes the future

holds not utopia, but a chilling vision of a society gone wrong. Writers turn to fantasy to escape their own world, but also to comment upon it. Thus Wells saw a perilous division of classes, Orwell an increasingly controlling state, and Atwood a world in which women have lost control of their bodies. At an all-too-real extreme, Bradbury envisioned books in flames. Still, aspects of the societies imagined by Gilman, or even Skinner, provide scenarios of a more rational future for readers to ponder.

The Time Machine (1895)

H(ERBERT) G(EORGE) WELLS (1866–1946)

The role of *The Time Machine* as a dystopian novel has been obscured by its fame as H. G. Wells's first science fiction novel and the one in which he invented the concept of the time machine.

Wells drew upon the ideas of many earlier theorists, including Charles Darwin, Simon Laplace, and Karl Marx, in composing this "scientific romance" with its subtle warning prophecy concerning the effects of rampant industrialization and continuing class discrimination. The seeming utopia in which the gentle Eloi (descendants of the upper classes) live in the year 802,701 is negated by the existence of the cannibalistic Morlocks (descendants of the lower classes). Those familiar only with the Hollywood movie have been deprived of Wells's apocalyptic vision: in the year 30,000,000, his Time Traveller witnesses an earth devoid of humanity under the fading light of a dying sun.

Der Judenstaat (1896)

{The Jewish State}

THEODOR HERZL (1860–1904)

Originally published in German in 1896, *Der Judenstaat* is the manifesto of Zionism, the modern political movement to establish a Jewish homeland.

From 1891 to 1895, Herzl was the Paris correspondent of the Viennese *Neue Freie Presse.* He was struck by the growth of anti-Semitism in France, where he covered the Dreyfus case, in which Alfred Dreyfus, a French officer and Jew, was wrongly convicted of treason and publicly stripped of his military rank. Herzl witnessed the rioting of the mob and heard the cries of "Death to the Jews." He concluded that the only solution was the mass resettlement of the Jews in a territory of their own.

In 1902, Herzl published a novel, *Altneuland* or *"Old New Land,"* a utopian fantasy of Jewish life, which he considered his greatest single literary achievement. According to Herzl's biographer, Ernst Pawel, the title, "rendered by Nahum Skolow, its Hebrew translator, as *Tel-Aviv (Hill of Spring),* has the distinction of having inspired the name of the first all-Jewish city of modern times." (See also Ezekiel 3:15.)

The Wonderful Wizard of Oz (1900)

L(YMAN) FRANK BAUM (1856–1919)

Nearly a century after this book's first publication, few Americans are unfamiliar with the image of Dorothy being carried by a Kansas cyclone into the magical land of Oz, where she meets the scarecrow, the tin woodman, and the cowardly lion. Their adventures looking for the Emerald City and the wizard have become a permanent part of American popular culture. Baum's work, originally self-published with striking illustrations by William Warren Denslow, was an immediate success with children; its popularity now is largely based on the 1939 film, starring Judy Garland as Dorothy.

In his introduction to the book, Baum argued that "the old-time fairy tale, having served for generations, may now be classed as 'historical'…the time has come for a series of newer 'wonder tales.'…Modern education includes morality, therefore the modern child needs only entertainment in its wonder-tales.…" *The Wonderful Wizard of Oz* lays claim to a place among the turning points in the secularization of American children's literature.

Peter Pan in Kensington Gardens (1906)

J(AMES) M(ATTHEW) BARRIE (1860–1937)

Peter Pan, "the boy who never grew up," appears in several of Barrie's works as the not quite mortal embodiment of the fantasy that recurs throughout his writing. He was actually a very real element in Barrie's own life; his playmates, the five young Davies brothers, inspired him to write the work, which Peter Llewelyn Davies was later to style "that terrible masterpiece." Peter's enduring popularity on stage and screen came mainly from his adventures with Wendy and Captain Hook. Barrie's twilight world of play with children and fairies in Kensington Gardens was brought to eerie life by the illustrations of Arthur Rackham, with which it is forever associated.

Herland (1915)

Charlotte Perkins Gilman (1860–1935)

From 1909 to 1916, Gilman published *The Forerunner,* a monthly women's rights magazine, which she also wrote and edited in its entirety. It was here that the "feminist-utopian" novel *Herland* first appeared, serialized in monthly installments.

"Lost" for more than 60 years, this tale of three young male adventurers and their encounters with the inhabitants of a prosperous country populated only by mothers and daughters was greeted with amusement and recognition when it was reprinted in 1979. One reviewer commented, "the conversations in which the visitors attempt to describe the outside world and its habits to the Amazons prickle with amusing jabs at the male-dominated society of 1915. Most of the jabs still find their target. . . ."

In her own time, Charlotte Perkins Gilman's considerable reputation rested on her commitment to promoting and melding socialist and feminist ideas.

Brave New World (1932)

ALDOUS HUXLEY (1894–1936)

This archetypal dystopian novel, set 600 years in the future, depicts a scientific and industrialized utopia in which mankind has sacrificed individuality to a world of abundant physical pleasures and material luxury. Conformity is maintained through the use of subliminal persuasion and a drug called "soma."

Universally regarded as a classic examination of 20th-century values, *Brave New World* remains as pertinent today as it was in 1932. Only 64 years later, such technological advances as test-tube babies, genetic engineering, and cloning are no longer impossible fantasies. Might the "brave new world" be possible? In the words of Huxley scholar Peter Firchow:

> The right response to Huxley's satire is not, or is not only, one of admiration at the brilliance of his literary imagination; it is one of horror at who we are and who, or rather what, we may become. The right response to *Brave New World* is to live our lives so as to prevent the coming of the brave new world....

Lost Horizon (1933)

James Hilton (1900–1954)

The age of air travel provides (ironically) the opportunity for a flight from reality and the evils of the modern world in this tale of an exotic community devoted to the calm contemplation of all that is most beautiful and representative of the highest ideals of civilization. Remote from our age of anxiety, in a fastness that protects its inhabitants even from the ravages of time, the book's Shangri-La eventually proves unattainable for the protagonist because of his human vulnerability.

Celebrated with the award of the Hawthornden Prize in 1934, and the basis for a Hollywood film in 1937, *Lost Horizon* made its most lasting contribution to our culture in "Shangri-La," a now-familiar term for a safe haven for the realization of one's ideals.

Walden Two (1948)

B. F. SKINNER (1904–1990)

One of the most controversial and influential figures in the field of psychology, B. F. Skinner was the chief proponent of the science of "radical behaviorism." This theory, which denies the existence of free will and suggests that human behavior is controlled solely by external environmental factors, dominated psychology from the 1930s through the 1960s.

Walden Two, Skinner's one work of fiction, portrays a utopian community in which positive and negative reinforcements are used to program approved behavior among its members. Reinforcement begins early: children are raised in communal nurseries and are taught proper thought patterns in school. The plot is minimal and serves merely as a framework within which Skinner's theories are debated.

Walden Two has been reprinted often and is required reading on many college campuses, where it remains the source of much debate. Several communes have been founded upon its guidelines.

Nineteen Eighty-four (1949)

George Orwell (Eric Arthur Blair) (1903–1950)

No other dystopian novel has received the critical acclaim or had the wide-ranging influence that *1984* has. Words and phrases such as "Big Brother is watching you," "doublethink," and "Orwellian" have become part of our language. The mere mention of "1984" conjures immediate images of a dystopian future. George Orwell succeeded beyond his wildest expectations in warning everyone of the dangers of a totalitarian society.

1984 has sold over 14 million English-language copies to date.

Fahrenheit 451 (1953)

RAY BRADBURY (b. 1920)

> Colored people don't like *Little Black Sambo*. Burn it.
> White people don't feel good about *Uncle Tom's Cabin*.
> Burn it. Someone's written a book on tobacco and cancer
> of the lungs? The cigarette people are weeping? Burn the
> book.

This classic dystopian novel on censorship contains many such incendiary and eerily prophetic passages. *Fahrenheit 451*, Bradbury's only full-length novel, is an expansion of a 1951 short story, "The Fireman," set in a near-future totalitarian state where books are outlawed and burned. The plot centers on the conversion of a "fireman" from book burner to book saver. The title of the novel refers to the temperature at which paper burns.

The book inspired a 1966 film by François Truffaut and a BBC symphony. *Fahrenheit 451* regularly appears on high school and college reading lists.

Atlas Shrugged (1957) *

AYN RAND (1905–1982)

Born Allyssa Rosenbaum in St. Petersburg, Ayn Rand lived through two Russian revolutions, the confiscation of her family's property, and years of deprivation before immigrating to the United States in 1926. Settling in Southern California, she worked in the motion picture industry and began to write in English.

Heroic egoism and the sovereignty of creative achievement were themes of her famous novel *The Fountainhead,* published in 1943. Fourteen years later came *Atlas Shrugged,* with its dark vision of a United States where industrial leaders have succumbed to strangulating government control.

In this polemic, religious altruism is coupled with 20th-century collectivist thought, and both are seen as destructive to the autonomy of the creative individual. For many readers, this argument came as a startling, liberating revelation. A *New Yorker* article noted that "As late as 1991,...a majority of Americans surveyed named *Atlas Shrugged* as the book that had most influenced their lives, after the Bible."

A Clockwork Orange (1962)

Anthony Burgess (John Anthony Burgess Wilson) (1917–1993)

A Clockwork Orange, his most popular and widely read book, is the "signature work" of Anthony Burgess, one of the most important contemporary novelists. This cacotopia (the term Burgess preferred to dystopia) gained critical attention in 1962 and became a campus cult classic in 1971 after Stanley Kubrick adapted it into an acclaimed film.

The most discussed aspect of this book is the slang Burgess created for his teenaged characters. Called "nadsat," it combines Cockney slang with Russian. Some critics considered it distracting and in questionable taste; others praised it for its emotional impact and the sense of reality it conveys.

A Clockwork Orange serves as a forum for the discussion of the nature of language and the conflicts between free will and determinism.

The Handmaid's Tale (1985)

MARGARET ATWOOD (b. 1939)

As John Updike wrote in his *New Yorker* review of this book, "Any futuristic novel, of course, is about the present: what has struck the writer as significant and ominous in the world now."

In the Republic of Gilead, religious extremists control the state and have imposed a totalitarian regime characterized by forced adherence to rigid sex roles. Homosexuals are hanged for the crime of Gender Treachery. Women are enslaved and are classified, according to their ability to reproduce, as "Handmaids," "Marthas," "Econowives," or even "Unwomen." All reading is forbidden to them, although women may listen as men read selected passages from the Bible.

The claustrophobic terror evoked by this book comes from taking common-enough prescriptions for gender-appropriate behavior to their logical conclusion.

War, Holocaust, Totalitarianism

The 20th century's crimes against humanity challenge our ability to speak. What words can capture the slaughter of millions? The feeling as a loved one, or a comrade, is murdered for a political cause? Here lies the triumph of writers in this section. As technology allowed modern states to pursue efficient and unprecedented programs of horror, individual voices bore witness. Anna Akhmatova defied Stalin's terror to lament her dead husband and imprisoned son. Siegfried Sassoon's poetry captured death (and sunsets) in the trenches. Hašek's Good Soldier

Schweik fought back with his wits. Even those separated by enemy lines found common ground in literature, as millions wept to Remarque's *All Quiet on the Western Front*. Literature offered hope: of memory, of future generations who would learn. Some writers hoped in vain, as John Reed envisioned a bright collective future. But above all it is chilling to remember the book that launched Hitler's programmatic destruction of the Jews. Yet, through the miracle of literature, a young girl's voice answers back.

Armenian Atrocities:
The Murder of a Nation (1915)

Arnold (Joseph) Toynbee (1889–1975)

Beginning in 1894, attempts had been made to exterminate the Armenians; in 1915, official Turkish efforts resulted in the deaths of more than 600,000 Armenians, either by murder by Turkish soldiers or through starvation during forced exile to Syria and Mesopotamia. Toynbee's book documented these brutalities and served to indict Turkish policy. This incident, along with his experience in Anatolia six years later, in 1921, when he chronicled Greek atrocities against Turks, led Toynbee to begin to investigate the relationship between such events and patterns of growth and decay of civilizations. These investigations resulted in Toynbee's *A Study of History* (1934–61), his best-known work.

Toynbee's contributions to this century's intellectual sphere, including his cross-cultural and global perspectives on history, made him one of the best-known, but often controversial, historians of his age.

Ten Days That Shook the World (1919)

John Reed (1887–1920)

Reed, an Oregonian who graduated from Harvard in 1910, produced vivid, partisan journalism about strikes in the American mining and textile industries and fought with Pancho Villa's rebels in northern Mexico before traveling to Russia in 1917. This, his famous pro-Bolshevik account of the October Revolution, was first published in March 1919. The book was endorsed by Lenin: "unreservedly do I recommend it to the workers of the world"; and Reed's friend Max Eastman even went so far as to claim that it "rises through timeliness and poetic heat and fidelity to fact into the realm of permanent literature." The book was suppressed by Stalin.

The War Poems (1919)

SIEGFRIED SASSOON (1886–1967)

Siegfried Sassoon and his direct counterparts, e.g., Wilfred Owen and Isaac Rosenberg, address their mutual experiences of war through a body of poetry which, though obviously differing in method and temperament, succeeds in portraying not only the futility of war but also how its victims endeavor to transcend its horror. Their poetry serves as an antidote to, and is in marked contrast with, the poetry of the romantic soldier-poets typified by Rupert Brooke.

The War Poems, which appeared in an edition of 2,000 copies in October 1919, gathers together appropriate poems from three previously published books as well as a few new ones. Sassoon's obituary in *The Times* of September 4, 1967, observed: "His angry *War Poems* had been the first to make him famous and he never quite achieved their pungency again." The collection remains one of the most noteworthy examples of its genre in modern literature.

Osudy dobrého vojáka Švejka za světové války (1920–23)

{The Good Soldier Schweik}

Jaroslav Hašek (1883–1923)

A universal folk character, the wise fool, is conscripted into the Austro-Hungarian army. In civilian life, Schweik made his living by forging pedigrees for the ugly mongrel dogs he sold to the unwary. In the army, he makes his way by candor and irony, serving as an orderly to such rear-guard officer types as a feckless, gambling-addicted chaplain and a womanizing lieutenant.

Satirizing both the Imperial Army and police-state tactics of Emperor Franz Joseph's security bureaucracy, this novel found great popularity with European audiences, who, in the 1920s, were prepared to acknowledge the futility of war. Originally written in Czech (Hašek was acquainted with Kafka), the book was quickly translated into German. A much-performed play and a successful movie followed. Inevitably, the book was banned and burned in Hitler's Germany.

The mordant illustrations by Joseph Lada are also famous.

Mein Kampf (1925)

ADOLF HITLER (1889–1945)

For leading a failed coup attempt in 1923, Adolf Hitler was imprisoned in Landsberg Fortress. There he wrote his autobiography, a rambling account of his development and his ideas. Before 1933, *Mein Kampf* sold a respectable 100,000 copies; by 1940, nearly six million copies had been sold, making the book Nazi Germany's number one best-seller. Sales swelled as gift editions were presented at retirements, all official occasions, and even, in special "bridal editions," at civil wedding ceremonies, so that the Führer's thoughts might "provide direction and be [a couple's] guiding star."

Winston Chuchill wrote, "When eventually [Hitler] came to power, there was no book which deserved more careful study from the rulers...of the Allied Powers. All was there — the programme of German resurrection; the technique of party propaganda...the rightful position of Germany at the summit of the world. Here was the new Koran of faith and war: turgid, verbose, shapeless, but pregnant with its message."

Im Westen nichts Neues (1928)
{All Quiet on the Western Front}

Erich Maria Remarque (1898–1970)

The title *All Quiet on the Western Front* is probably better remembered than is the name of its author, Erich Maria Remarque. First serialized in 1928 in the *Vossische Zeitung,* it appeared in book form the next year in German and numerous other languages. An immediate best-seller, it was adapted as a motion picture in 1930. Paul Bäumer, its principal character, has since become an everyman icon in antiwar literature and cinema.

Equally important, the novel is an indictment of a "civilization" that could descend to such warfare with its anomic consequences. It stands in contrast, for example, to Ernst Jünger's *In Stahlgewittern* (1920), which also saw its first English translation in 1929, as *Storm of Steel; from the Diary of a German Storm-Troop Officer on the Western Front.* The latter captured yet another mood and other possibilities which ultimately—and with historical irony—enabled Goebbels to consign *Im Westen nichts Neues* to the flames in 1933.

Rekviem (1935–40)
{Requiem}

ANNA AKHMATOVA (ANNA ANDREEVNA GORENKO) (1889–1966)

At the height of the Stalinist Terror, Russian poet Anna Akhmatova—already a powerful voice for her generation—began a cycle of poems called *Requiem.* In constant danger and prohibited from publishing, Akhmatova nonetheless refused to emigrate. *Requiem* was whispered from friend to friend, until a first edition appeared in Munich in 1963, without the knowledge of the poet herself. A record of her personal suffering following the death of her husband and the imprisonment of her son, *Requiem* is also one of the century's great poems of witness.

Joseph Brodsky has written of *Requiem,* "At certain periods of history it is only poetry that is capable of dealing with reality by condensing it into something graspable, something that otherwise couldn't be retained by the mind. In that sense, the whole nation took up the pen name of Akhmatova...."

For Whom the Bell Tolls (1940)

ERNEST HEMINGWAY (1899–1961)

This novel of the Spanish Civil War was Hemingway's most ambitious artistic endeavor as well as his greatest popular success. The story of Robert Jordan, a young American committed to the Loyalist cause, it is notable for Hemingway's evocative prose style. The epigraph, taken from one of Donne's sermons, suggests the work's universal implications. "Very likely," wrote Philip Young, "there is no country in which American books are read whose literature has been entirely unaffected by Hemingway's work. In his own country we are so conditioned to his influence that we stopped noticing it some time ago, and seldom stop to realize that the story we are reading might have been quite different, or not written at all, except for him."

Darkness at Noon (1941)

ARTHUR KOESTLER (1905–1983)

Arthur Koestler's own experience as a foreign correspondent in Spain and the Soviet Union, and as a member of the German Communist party, resulted in his novel *Darkness at Noon,* best described in Koestler's dedication:

> The characters in this book are fictitious. The historical circumstances which determined their actions are real. The life of the man N. S. Rubashov is a synthesis of the lives of a number of men who were victims of the so-called Moscow Trials. Several of them were personally known to the author. This book is dedicated to their memory. *Paris, October 1938 – April 1940.*

Reviewing the book in *The New Statesman and Nation,* George Orwell observed, "Brilliant as this book is as a novel, and a piece of prison literature, it is probably most valuable as an interpretation of the Moscow 'confessions' by someone with an inner knowledge of totalitarian methods."

Hiroshima (1946)

JOHN HERSEY (1914–1993)

Fifty years have passed since atomic bombs fell on the Japanese cities of Hiroshima and Nagasaki. This simply written account of the lives of six survivors in the months after the explosion was first published in the August 31, 1946, issue of *The New Yorker*, with the following statement from the editors:

> The New Yorker this week devotes its entire editorial space to an article on the almost complete obliteration of a city by one atomic bomb, and what happened to the people of that city. It does so in the conviction that few of us have yet comprehended the all but incredible destructive power of this weapon, and that everyone might well take time to consider the terrible implications of its use.

Het Achterhuis (1947)
{The Diary of a Young Girl}

ANNE FRANK (1929–1945)

When postwar German audiences saw films of concentration camps, according to one Berlin newspaper, they jeered in "derision and disbelief." When subsequent German audiences watched the stage dramatization of *The Diary of Anne Frank*, they "were so stunned they remained in their seats five minutes after the final curtain fell." Such is the power of the testimony of this young girl, who described two years hiding from the Nazis in Holland. Anne Frank named her diary "Kitty," and in its pages recorded the routines of eight people sharing desperate quarters. As she confided her first love, her ambitions, and her fears in a voice of increasing maturity, Frank captured a human loss that no statistics can measure.

The hiding place was raided in August 1944, and Frank died of typhoid fever at the Bergen-Belsen concentration camp in March 1945. Her diary was published by her father to lasting acclaim in 1947, as *Het Achterhuis* (literally, "The House Behind"). It was reissued in 1995, unexpurgated.

The Gathering Storm (1948)

Winston Churchill (1874–1965)

This first volume of Churchill's monumental history, *The Second World War* (6 vols., 1948–54), describes the failure of diplomacy and democracy to heal the wounds left by the war of 1914–18 and to prevent the remilitarization and subsequent aggressions of Germany. Churchill drew upon thousands of his own memoranda and documents in British archives, but in the end, this epic is structured on his personal experiences and expresses his courage and astonishing self-confidence.

This volume ends with Churchill's acquiring the "chief power in the State," on May 10, 1940, with his appointment as Prime Minister. He remembers, "During these last crowded days of political crisis, my pulse had not quickened at any moment, I took it all as it came. But I cannot conceal from the reader of this truthful account that as I went to bed at about 3 a.m., I was conscious of a profound sense of relief. At last I had the authority to give directions over the entire scene."

La nuit (1958)*
{Night}

ELIE WIESEL (b. 1928)

> Never shall I forget those moments which murdered my
> God and my soul and turned my dreams to dust. Never
> shall I forget these things, even if I am condemned to live
> as long as God, himself. Never.

Elie Wiesel voiced these lamentations after a decade of
self-imposed silence about his experiences in Auschwitz
and Buchenwald. His memoir began as a manuscript of
over 800 pages, written in Yiddish. With the encourage-
ment of François Mauriac, Wiesel abridged and concen-
trated the work to 127 harrowing pages for publication in
French. The poet A. Alvarez writes that "Wiesel's pain
lies in the discovery that neither love, filial piety, nor his
intense Talmudic training can stand up against extremes
of starvation and fear....As a human document, Night is
almost unbearably painful, and certainly beyond criticism."

Wiesel has received scores of prizes and awards for both
literary achievement and humanitarian advocacy, most
notably the Nobel Peace Prize in 1986.

Quotations from Chairman Mao (1966)

MAO ZEDONG (1893–1976)

The "Little Red Book" was the fetish object of China's Cultural Revolution. Hundreds of millions of copies were distributed in the 1960s, first to soldiers of the People's Liberation Army, then to the rampaging teenagers who formed the Red Guard, and finally to ardent would-be Maoists throughout the world.

Mao had been in semi-seclusion after the failure in 1959 of his Great Leap Forward. The publication of this tiny volume, thought to be the work of Defense Minister Lin Biao, who culled bits and pieces from Mao's speeches and political writings, heralded the Party Chairman's return. Responding to Mao's exhortation to "knock down the old," the Red Guard mobs did their worst, each individual brandishing a copy of the "Little Red Book."

The book continues to be satirized today with the publication of such titles as *Quotations from Speaker Newt.*

Bury My Heart at Wounded Knee: An Indian History of the American West (1970)

DEE ALEXANDER BROWN (b. 1908)

A number one nonfiction best-seller in 1971, this well-documented narrative focuses on the 30-year period, 1860 – 90, in the history of the American West during which the last resisting tribes were defeated in the worst Indian wars fought for possession of land.

The popularity of this book was due partly to renewed interest in American Indian issues and partly to the parallels between the events described in the book and the brutal actions of the military at My Lai, Vietnam, in 1968, which shocked the nation. Written from the viewpoint of the Indians, this unusual book is based primarily on records of treaty councils, diaries, pictographic records, autobiographies, and other primary sources.

Included are the words of such Indian leaders as Chief Joseph, Geronimo, and Crazy Horse.

Arkhipelag GULag, 1918–1956 (1973–75)

{The Gulag Archipelago, 1918–1956: An Experiment in Literary Investigation}

Aleksandr I(sayevich) Solzhenitsyn
(b. 1918)

Aleksandr Solzhenitsyn is regarded as the greatest living Russian novelist, continuing the tradition of 19th-century masters such as Tolstoy or Dostoyevsky. His novels are known and read all over the world, and he was awarded the Nobel Prize in Literature in 1970. Yet his name is often associated with a work of nonfiction: *The Gulag Archipelago,* a historical account based in part on his own imprisonment in Stalin's labor camps from 1945 to 1953.

This detailed and comprehensive testimony of the cruelty and injustice of the Soviet system was written as a tribute to that system's countless victims. In 1973, it was smuggled out of the country and published in Paris. A year later, Solzhenitsyn was expelled from the Soviet Union.

Dispatches (1977)

MICHAEL HERR (b. 1940)

As a young correspondent for *Esquire* magazine, Herr reported on the undeclared war in Vietnam. His articles, which are the basis of this book, began to appear after the Tet Offensive, launched by the National Liberation Front in January 1968 when about 500,000 American troops were in Vietnam. Herr depicts the day-to-day reality of these young soldiers, many of whom were teenaged draftees, using their own defiant, hallucinatory vocabulary. In *The New York Times Book Review*, C.D.B. Bryan asserted that "Quite simply, *Dispatches* is the best book to have been written about the Vietnam War"; but Paul Gray claimed in *Time* that "Herr dared to travel to that irrational place and to come back with the worst imaginable news: war thrives because enough men still love it."

Michael Herr went on to co-write the screenplays for *Apocalypse Now* (1979) and *Full Metal Jacket* (1988).

Maus: A Survivor's Tale (1986–91)

ART SPIEGELMAN (b. 1947)

Maus: A Survivor's Tale is a unique title in the literature of the Holocaust. In comic-strip (or graphic novel) format, Spiegelman chronicles his father's experiences in Poland and, later, in German-run concentration camps during World War II; the Jews are depicted as mice and the Germans as cats. Maus also considers the effects of those experiences upon the lives of the next generation.

Maus was published in 1986 and won instant acclaim from the literary community, the Jewish community, and the general public. Maus II appeared in 1991. Subsequently, it was awarded a Special Pulitzer Prize and the National Book Critics Circle Award, among many other honors.

Spiegelman's unique contribution to Holocaust literature was aptly described by Lawrence L. Langer, writing in The New York Times: "Perhaps no Holocaust narrative will ever contain the whole experience. But Art Spiegelman has found an original and authentic form to draw us closer to its bleak heart."

OPTIMISM, JOY, GENTILITY

he world can be dark and unpredictable, and literature often captures those somber tones. But literature can also create a world apart, offering what Robert Frost called "a momentary stay against confusion." The writers in this section affirm the possibility of joy in life, and in literature. They celebrate the small pleasures, from Pooh's jar of honey to Jeeves's impeccable attire. They articulate the manners that help us live together — a gift for which we might cordially thank Emily Post. They guide us through daily rituals, as Shaw contemplated the art

of speaking, and Mrs. Rombauer "the joy of cooking." A few special books create spaces to which we return again and again for solace, from the *Goodnight Moon* room, to the Hobbit's hole, to *The Country of the Pointed Firs.* Optimistic books don't necessarily ignore life's dark side: Harper Lee's *To Kill a Mockingbird* captured a racially torn South, and Helen Keller knew isolation and despair firsthand. But writers in this section made a brighter world as they informed, delighted—and offered hope.

The Country of the Pointed Firs (1896)

SARAH ORNE JEWETT (1849–1909)

"The distinction and refinement of Sarah Jewett's prose," wrote Francis O. Matthiessen, "came out of an America which, with its Tweed Rings and grabbing Trusts, its blatantly moneyed New York and squalid frontier towns, seemed most lacking in just these qualities."

A fishing village on the coast of Maine is the scene of this beautifully crafted novel. A summer visitor comes to lodge in the tiny, secluded house of an herbalist who heals the sick with medicines she brews from her "rustic pharmacopoeia." The novel affirms the dignity and integrity of these two women and, indeed, of all the characters. The isolated rural people in particular are shown to possess an ennobling sense of their place in nature and in history.

Sometimes disparaged for writing "local color" fiction, in *The Country of the Pointed Firs,* Jewett transcended regionalism to produce a novel that Willa Cather ranked with *The Scarlet Letter* and *The Adventures of Huckleberry Finn.*

The Story of My Life (1903)

HELEN KELLER (1880–1968)

Published in 1903, the year before her graduation from Radcliffe College, *The Story of My Life* describes Helen Keller's early life and, especially, her work with Anne Sullivan, from the epiphany of rediscovering words at the age of seven — "Suddenly I felt a misty consciousness as of something forgotten—a thrill of returning thought; and somehow the mystery of language was revealed to me."— to learning how to read, write, and speak, skills she had lost when an illness left her blind, deaf, and mute at 19 months. Though Mark Twain described her as one of the two most interesting people of the 19th century (the other being Napoleon), Helen Keller was very much of the 20th century. In addition to writing, she lectured and supported such causes as peace, women's suffrage, and birth control. But the cause for which she is most celebrated—and which took her to the White House to meet with every President from Grover Cleveland to John F. Kennedy — was that of improving conditions for people who are blind.

The Innocence of Father Brown (1911)

G(ILBERT) K(EITH) CHESTERTON
(1874–1936)

A prolific belletrist, G. K. Chesterton enjoyed paradox. His most admired literary creation was an unassuming little priest who was also a cunning and resourceful detective. Chesterton explained, "In Father Brown, it was the chief feature to be featureless....His commonplace exterior was meant to contrast with his unsuspected vigilance and intelligence." Father Brown often solves crimes not by doggedly following clues, but by combining intuition with charity, knowing the hearts of men, identifying with the criminals and bringing them to recognition and repentance.

Few literary genres have given readers as much pleasure as the detective novel. In Father Brown, Chesterton invented one of the first of many fictional mystery-solvers whose involvement with the world of crime is startlingly incongruent with their vocation. And although the character is a priest, he "fathered" such offspring as Harry Kemelman's Rabbi David Small and Ellis Peters's Brother Cadfael.

Platero y Yo (1914)

{Platero and I; An Andalusian Elegy}

JUAN RAMÓN JIMÉNEZ (1881–1958)

This book graces childhood in Spanish-speaking house-holds throughout the world. A prose-poem and a master-piece, it was an early success of Juan Ramón Jiménez, who was awarded the Nobel Prize in Literature in 1956.

The book chronicles the wanderings over a single year of Platero, a small, hairy donkey "with a gay little trot like laughter," and the beast's contemplative master. The pair travel through the stark and fabled countryside of the province of Andalusia in southern Spain, encountering its peasants, gypsies, and sweet, vivacious children. The critic Michael Predmore noted regretfully that much of the commentary this work has attracted is "sheer eulogy," because the book is not the simple, lyric tale it at first appears to be. A closer reading shows that it also contains "ritual elements in a great seasonal drama" and thus becomes a profound meditation on the universal themes of death, rebirth, and resurrection.

Pygmalion (1914)

GEORGE BERNARD SHAW (1856–1950)

Pygmalion, first performed in England in 1914, became one of Shaw's most popular plays, and has been enjoyed in many incarnations (film, Broadway musical, film *of* Broadway musical). But the romantic denouement of these later treatments distorts Shaw's own ironic ending. The story of a Cockney flower-seller, Eliza Doolittle, trained to pass as a lady by a phonetician, Henry Higgins, certainly generates romantic expectations, but Shaw's distinctive sensibility leaves them unsettled. Although the play is based upon the classical legend of Pygmalion, who fell in love with his own sculpture, Shaw has, according to David J. Gordon, "individualised his characters to a remarkable degree and dramatised their story with exceptional intimacy and directness," creating in this work his "major achievement in the mode of the anti-sublime."

Etiquette in Society, in Business, in Politics, and at Home (1922)

EMILY (PRICE) POST (1872–1960)

To wealth and good manners born, Emily Price Post became a professional writer out of necessity after a divorce. Enjoying a fruitful career in fiction and journalism, she was persuaded, as a successful writer and former debutante, to do a book on etiquette for Americans.

Emily Post's "Blue Book" brought her immediate fame and authority as an arbiter of correct behavior. She stressed simplicity, consideration, and common sense in social affairs: the basic principle of making the other person comfortable. Etiquette is conservative by definition, but Emily Post was responsive to change, and the ten editions of *Etiquette* that appeared during her lifetime reflect the social history of—especially—the American middle class.

In a serious moment she once wrote, "Etiquette is the science of living. It embraces everything. It is the code of sportsmanship and of honor. It is ethics."

The Inimitable Jeeves (1923)

P(ELHAM) G(RENVILLE) WODEHOUSE (1881–1975)

How is it possible to select just one of the 90-some Wodehouse books? He published his first in 1910 and was working on his last when he died in 1975, and was thus a contemporary of both Thomas Hardy and Norman Mailer. The ageless Bertie Wooster and Jeeves first appeared in *The Inimitable Jeeves*; they continue to live in a sort of timeless Edwardian high summer.

As Evelyn Waugh has written, "All [of Wodehouse's characters] exist in a world of pristine paradisal innocence. For Mr. Wodehouse there has been no Fall of Man....His characters have never tasted the forbidden fruit. They are still in Eden....Mr. Wodehouse's idyllic world can never stale. He will continue to release future generations from captivity that may be more irksome than our own. He has made a world for us to live in and delight in."

Winnie-the-Pooh (1926)

A(LAN) A(LEXANDER) MILNE (1882–1956)

Milne, an assistant editor of *Punch* and a writer of novels, plays, and essays, achieved his lasting fame in writing for children. Creating scenes of solemn whimsy whose gentle humor appeals to young and old alike, Milne realized his nostalgia for the Arcadia of childhood through the imagined sayings and doings of his son's nursery toys. The enduring charm of Milne's stories comes from the child-like simplicity of events, characters, and conversations; by contrast, the only human character, the child Christopher Robin, is endowed with godlike stature and understanding. An indispensable part of the appeal are the illustrations by Ernest A. Shepard, whose understated wit successfully captures the spirit of this and other Christopher Robin books.

Shadows on the Rock (1931)

WILLA CATHER (1875–1947)

Set in Quebec in 1697, this small, serene novel about a 12-year-old girl who keeps house for her father, a widowed apothecary, describes a year in the life of Cecile and Euclide Auclair, whose orderly and loving household is protected from the vast Canadian wilderness by the civic and religious institutions of Kebec, the "Rock."

In 1931, when as many as five million American workers were jobless and the industrializing world seemed about to collapse, the relatively stable traditional community depicted in this beautifully written novel provided solace to its readers. It was the first of Willa Cather's many books to become a best-seller.

The Joy of Cooking: A Compilation of Reliable Recipes with a Casual Culinary Chat (1931)

IRMA S. ROMBAUER (1877–1962)

After her husband's death, Irma Rombauer was urged to publish the trove of never-fail recipes and techniques she had been collecting since her marriage. Her approach was reason and clarity, peppered with witty asides on culinary matters. Mrs. Rombauer's classic — in its first, privately published edition a modest volume of 395 pages, 500 recipes — went on to become the best-selling cookbook in publishing history. Editions from 1943 on incorporated her famous step-by-step method; the third revision, with her daughter, Marion Rombauer Becker, offered up 4,000 recipes in 1,000+ pages.

Noting that after her death, subsequent editions were heavily revised, James Beard observed that "Irma Rombauer is one of the great women of American cookery and deserves to be known in her original state of joy."

The Hobbit, or There and Back Again (1937)

J(OHN) R(ONALD) R(EUEL) TOLKIEN (1892–1973)

In enchanted Middle-earth, a small, comfort-loving Hobbit is awakened from his slumbers by a visitor who tells of lost treasure. Before Bilbo Baggins returns home again, he journeys past wizards and elves, talkative trees and treasure-guarding dragons, all swirling in cosmic battle between good and evil. J.R.R. Tolkien's fully realized fantasy world won over generations of children, and dazzled adults with its deft interweaving of medieval legend and made-up languages, maps, and creatures. In publishing the bedtime stories he told his children, Tolkien legitimized the modern fantasy genre, and provided the 1960s counterculture with antiwar, back-to-Eden icons.

Tolkien, who taught Old and Middle English at Oxford University, followed *The Hobbit* with the even more popular *Lord of the Rings* trilogy. C. S. Lewis, who had persuaded Tolkien to publish *The Hobbit,* described "the silvan leafiness, the passions, the high virtues, the remote horizons," as "surely the utmost reach of invention."

Goodnight Moon (1947)

MARGARET WISE BROWN (1910–1952)

Few books have been as cherished as *Goodnight Moon.* Night after night, the youngest children—and their parents, too—grow happily sleepy to the poetry of a world at rest. The illustrations by Clement Hurd remain vivid after half a century. Do you remember finding the mouse in each new picture?

Margaret Wise Brown saved nursery-age readers from publishing industry "neglect." She said: "A book can make a child laugh or feel clear-and-happy-headed as he follows a simple rhythm to its logical end. It can jog him with the unexpected and comfort him with the familiar, lift him for a few minutes from his own problems of shoelaces that won't tie and busy parents and mysterious clock-time, into the world of a bug or a bear or a bee or a boy living in the timeless world of story." During her short life, Brown wrote more than 100 books for children.

To Kill a Mockingbird (1960)

HARPER LEE (b. 1926)

Published during the interval between the Montgomery Bus Boycott (1955) and the March on Washington (1963), this singular novel of life in a small south Alabama town was a national best-seller and won the Pulitzer Prize for Fiction.

The narrator is Scout Finch, a precocious eight-year-old girl. She loves her widowed father, Atticus, although she considers him "feeble" as he is almost 50 and avoids football and shooting guns. But as Scout weaves her tale, combining childhood lore, the half-understood conversations of neighborhood adults, and her own vivid impressions, the pattern of her father's heroism emerges and the unsuspected courage of several other characters, both black and white, is revealed.

The film adaptation, released in 1962, was also a critical success, earning Academy Awards for Horton Foote, who wrote the screenplay, and for Gregory Peck, in the role of Atticus.

The Best of Simple (1961)

LANGSTON HUGHES (1902–1967)

Jesse B. Semple, folk-philosopher and abundantly inventive *raconteur*, made his first appearance in 1943 as a character in a newspaper column written by Langston Hughes for the black-owned *Chicago Defender*. Years later, beginning with *Simple Speaks His Mind* (1950), a series of books brought this unforgettable personality to a larger, racially mixed audience.

Semple is a hardworking Harlemite whose humorous sayings and trenchant views are captured for readers by his staid and conventional drinking partner. Richard Barksdale argues that in the characterization of Semple, Hughes, the great poet of the Harlem Renaissance, puts forth his own hard-won "socially salutary comic view proclaiming that out of the complexities of modern urban living and the mountainous mass of human error, 'simple' men will emerge to pronounce 'simple' truths."

The Complete Poems, 1927–1979 (1983)

ELIZABETH BISHOP (1911–1979)

Among the strident and garrulous poetic voices of her generation, Elizabeth Bishop was famously reticent, and her "output" was not large: the complete poems barely reach 150. But the voice is absolutely like no other before or since, each poem, in the words of Octavio Paz, "as perfect as a cat or a rose."

Elizabeth Bishop grew up in Massachusetts and Nova Scotia. Her father had died and her mother gone mad (the scream heard through the short story "In the Village") by the time she was four. "Wide, haphazard reading" was her early education. After graduating from Vassar in 1934, she began the life of travel — to Europe, Florida, Brazil, and other ports of call — that became a central metaphor of her writing. She died in Boston in 1979.

The experience of poetry seems never so private nor so total as in reading Elizabeth Bishop. One is drawn utterly into her imaginative universe, to the strangeness at the heart of the everyday world: a mysterious and unsettling rapture — "like what we imagine knowledge to be."

FAVORITES OF CHILDHOOD AND YOUTH

My first book—held in my 3-year-old hands—was tiny, beautiful *Peter Rabbit*. I knew it was an important part of my life," wrote a visitor to the exhibition. Lucky people have such memories. Books written for children and adolescents often resonate for a lifetime. Who can forget the menace of Mr. McGregor's garden; Charlotte's plot to exempt Wilbur from the prevailing fate of pigs; the Queen of Narnia tempting a small adventurer with Turkish Delight; Max's dream romp in his wolf suit; or Holden Caulfield's anxious quest? Whether set in fantasy

worlds or the gritty particularity of Francie Nolan's Brooklyn, these wonderful books all feature heroes and heroines — some tentative, shy, even foolish — who put aside their fears and venture forth from home (a little boy explores a neighborhood transformed by snow, Sarah Wheaton travels westward from the coast of Maine, and even Wilbur is carted up for a visit to the county fair). Such journeys comprise a universal metaphor of, and perhaps consolation for, growing up.

The Tale of Peter Rabbit (1902)

(Helen) Beatrix Potter (1866–1943)

A letter written in 1893 to the son of her former governess led to the birth of the bunny who defines the term "classic" in children's stories. Peter, who would appear in print in 1902, never loses his rabbitness while coming to symbolize that eternal truth of human childhood — naughtiness. Anne Carroll Moore, the first superintendent of work with children at The New York Public Library, wrote that "Far and few were the new books for little children at the turn of the century. Here was one of such exceptional quality and charm that it could be shared on equal terms with the head of the art department...and the children to whom I first read it aloud...." In a heartfelt tribute from one artist to another, Maurice Sendak described how Potter drew from "careful observation of her subject. And how she could draw!...*Peter Rabbit*, for all its gentle tininess, loudly proclaims that no story is worth the writing, no picture worth the making, if it is not a work of imagination."

When all the commercial Peter novelties are consigned to a historical trash heap, this little book will remain in every child's heart.

A Tree Grows in Brooklyn (1943)

BETTY SMITH (1896–1972)

Forty years before Holden Caulfield abandoned Pencey Prep to begin his ill-fated Manhattan odyssey, Francie Nolan struggled to obtain an education in the teeming tenement neighborhood of Williamsburg, Brooklyn. Francie grows up nurtured by the loving gallantries of her father, a singing waiter who drinks too much, and the rigorous austerities practiced by her brave mother, a janitress who reads to her children each night from the complete plays of Shakespeare and the "Protestant Bible."

Betty Smith claimed that the catalyst for her semi-autobiographical novel was Thomas Wolfe's *Of Time and the River.* "I read it and all of Brooklyn came back like a flood." Her book was an instant best-seller, with 300,000 copies purchased in its first six weeks. Writing in the *Yale Review,* Orville Prescott praised *A Tree Grows in Brooklyn* as a "rich and rare example of regional local color writing, filled to the scuppers with Brooklynese, Brooklyn folkways and Brooklyn atmosphere."

The Lion, the Witch and the Wardrobe (1950)

C(LIVE) S(TAPLES) LEWIS (1898–1963)

In a letter to one of his many fans, the Oxford and Cambridge professor of English language and literature said of himself: "I'm tall, fat, rather bald, red-faced, double-chinned, black-haired, have a deep voice, and wear glasses for reading." He was also a passionate champion of Christianity and the creator of a folkloric kingdom called Narnia. Four English children first entered this world of good and evil through a door in a cupboard in 1950's *The Lion, the Witch and the Wardrobe*. Their story ends with the seventh title in the series, *The Last Battle*. "Narnia is a world of excitement and adventure, full of unexpected characters whom we cannot forget when once we have met with them," wrote Roger Lancelyn Green in *Tellers of Tales*. But it is not only the mystical Aslan the Lion or the evil White Witch who remain in our imagination; it is also the children in the tales, as ordinary as those who still treasure the stories.

The Catcher in the Rye (1951)

J(EROME) D(AVID) SALINGER (b. 1919)

With *The Catcher in the Rye,* J. D. Salinger introduced a new sort of character to modern American literature: the alienated adolescent. Intelligent, but unable to study; attractive, but unable to maintain friendships; lonely, but unable to ask for love, Holden Caulfield is a troubled youth who obviously needs help. With his excellent ear for dialogue, the author allowed Holden to speak and think as teens really do, four letter words and all. The plot covers two days in the teen's life when he leaves his prep school and wanders in New York City instead of going home. His sophistication disappears as he becomes sicker both physically and emotionally until his little sister is able to help him.

When the novel appeared in 1951, it was shocking. *The New York Herald Tribune Book Review* stated, "recent war novels have accustomed us all to ugly words and images, but from the mouths of the very young and protected they sound peculiarly offensive." Today's readers recognize Holden as a youthful rebel against adult authority.

Charlotte's Web (1952)

E(LWYN) B(ROOKS) WHITE (1899–1985)

In this classic work, E.B. White's profound respect for the English language and his farmer's regard for all living forms come together in the tale of the friendship between Wilbur the pig and Charlotte the wise spider, who formulates a plan to save his life. Published in 1952 to great critical acclaim, *Charlotte's Web* immediately attained classic status as a story of the cycle of life and death. Garth Williams's drawings personified the endearing personalities and are an integral component of the beauty of the book.

Eudora Welty wrote in *The New York Times* that this book "is just about perfect, and just magical in the way it is done." With more than six million copies sold in more than 18 languages, it appears that children and adults are in perfect agreement.

The Snowy Day (1962)

Ezra Jack Keats (1916–1983)

When a little boy named Peter first put on his red snowsuit and made tracks in the snow, a whole new world of children's book illustration began. Keats was remembering his own happy times playing in the snow, and decided to write a story about them. But Peter did not look like the typical little boy seen in picture books, for Keats's inspiration was a 1940 photograph from LIFE magazine of an African American child.

The Snowy Day was awarded the Caldecott Medal in 1963 for its striking collage design, which featured bright colors and fabrics ranging from a rare Belgian linen to oilcloth. Keats wrote that he "wanted the world to know that all children experience wonderful things in life. I wanted to convey the joy of being a little boy alive on a certain kind of day—of being for that moment."

Where the Wild Things Are (1963)

MAURICE SENDAK (b. 1928)

"Wild Things!" When Max's sojourn among them unfolded in kinematic splendor in 1963, adults trembled and children reveled. Reaching back into his own Brooklyn childhood, Sendak created the enduring child-hero Max, who overcomes his fears and achieves catharsis in a colorful fantasy tableau.

Where the Wild Things Are was awarded the 1964 Caldecott Medal by the American Library Association. In his acceptance speech, Sendak paid homage to the picture books of his muse, Randolph Caldecott. "The action is paced to the beat of a perky march, a comic fugue, and an English country dance — I can hear the music as I turn the pages." Children still thrill to the beat of the "wild rumpus," and opera companies perform it worldwide for adults who are no longer fretful.

Sarah, Plain and Tall (1985)

PATRICIA MACLACHLAN (b. 1938)

Recipe for American Family Pie

Ingredients:

- 1 mail-order bride from Maine
- 1 widowed father
- 2 motherless children

Utensils: 1 prairie home

Directions:

Mix all ingredients with a large quantity of love and a pinch of homesickness for the Atlantic Ocean.

- Bake in a prairie-style oven until firm.
- Serve 1 chapter each evening until done.

In her review in *The Horn Book,* Ethel L. Heins wrote that this "brief, well-rounded tale has its own satisfying completeness." In her Newbery acceptance speech, MacLachlan said that she "wished to write my mother's story with spaces, like the prairie, with silences that could say what words could not."

Not surprisingly, this beautiful family love story was brought to the TV screen as a Hallmark Hall of Fame production, starring Glenn Close.

First Editions

This list gives the first appearance in book form of the Books of the Century. Earlier periodical appearances are cited only when book publication did not occur for a number of years. Readers should note that in the text, the year of publication given is that of first appearance in print, in any format.

Chinua Achebe. *Things Fall Apart*. London: Heinemann, 1958.

Henry Adams. *The Education of Henry Adams*. Washington, D.C.: Privately printed, 1907.

Jane Addams. *Twenty Years at Hull-House*. New York: Macmillan, 1910.

James Agee and Walker Evans. *Let Us Now Praise Famous Men*. Boston: Houghton Mifflin, 1941.

Anna Akhmatova. *Rekviem {Requiem}*. Munich: Tvorchestvo zarubezhnykh pisatelei, 1963. [First publication of poems written 1935–40.]

Maya Angelou. *I Know Why the Caged Bird Sings*. New York: Random House, 1969.

Margaret Atwood. *The Handmaid's Tale*. Toronto: McClelland and Stewart, 1985.

W. H. Auden. *The Age of Anxiety: A Baroque Eclogue*. New York: Random House, 1947.

James Baldwin. *The Fire Next Time*. New York: Dial Press, 1963.

J. M. Barrie. *Peter Pan in Kensington Gardens*. Drawings by Arthur Rackham. London: Hodder & Stoughton, 1906.

L. Frank Baum. *The Wonderful Wizard of Oz*. Chicago and New York: G. M. Hill, 1900.

Simone de Beauvoir. *Le deuxième sexe {The Second Sex}*. 2 vols. Paris: Gallimard, 1949.

Samuel Beckett. *En attendant Godot: pièce en deux actes {Waiting for Godot: A Tragicomedy in Two Acts}*. Paris: Editions de Minuit, 1952.

Bruno Bettelheim. *The Uses of Enchantment*. New York: Knopf, 1976.

The Holy Bible. Revised Standard Version. New York: T. Nelson, 1952.

Elizabeth Bishop. *The Complete Poems, 1927 – 1979*. New York: Farrar Straus Giroux, 1983.

Jorge Luis Borges. *Ficciones (1935 – 1944) {Fictions}*. Buenos Aires: Sur, 1944.

Jim Bouton. *Ball Four: My Life and Hard Times Throwing the Knuckleball in the Big Leagues*. Edited by Leonard Shecter. New York: World Publishing Company, 1970.

Ray Bradbury. *Fahrenheit 451*. New York: Ballantine Books, 1953.

Dee Alexander Brown. *Bury My Heart at Wounded Knee: An Indian History of the American West*. New York: Holt, Rinehart & Winston, 1970.

Margaret Wise Brown. *Goodnight Moon*. Pictures by Clement Hurd. New York: Harper & Row, 1947.

Susan Brownmiller. *Against Our Will: Men, Women and Rape*. New York: Simon and Schuster, 1975.

Anthony Burgess. *A Clockwork Orange*. London: Heinemann, 1962.

Edgar Rice Burroughs. *Tarzan of the Apes*. Chicago: A. C. McClurg, 1914.

Albert Camus. *L'étranger: roman {The Stranger}*. Paris: Gallimard, 1942.

Truman Capote. *In Cold Blood: A True Account of a Multiple Murder and Its Consequences*. New York: Random House, 1965.

Dale Carnegie. *How to Win Friends and Influence People*. New York: Simon and Schuster, 1936.

Rachel Carson. *Silent Spring*. Boston and Cambridge, Mass.: Houghton Mifflin; Riverside Press, 1962.

Willa Cather. *Shadows on the Rock*. New York: Knopf, 1931.

Carrie Chapman Catt and Nettie Rogers Shuler. *Woman Suffrage and Politics: The Inner Story of the Suffrage Movement*. New York: Charles Scribner's Sons, 1923.

Raymond Chandler. *The Big Sleep*. New York: Knopf, 1939.

Anton Chekhov. *Tri sestry {The Three Sisters}*. *Russkaia mysl'*, no. 2 (1901), pp. 124–78.

G. K. Chesterton. *The Innocence of Father Brown*. London and New York: Cassell, 1911.

Agatha Christie. *The Mysterious Affair at Styles*. New York and London: John Lane, 1920.

Winston Churchill. *The Gathering Storm*. Volume 1 of his *The Second World War*. London: Cassell, 1948.

Arthur Conan Doyle. *The Hound of the Baskervilles*. Illustrated by Sidney Paget. London: George Newnes, 1902.

Joseph Conrad. *Lord Jim.* Edinburgh and London: William Blackwood and Sons, 1900.

Marie Sklodowska Curie. *Traité de radioactivité {Treatise on Radioactivity}.* 2 vols. Paris: Gauthier-Villars, 1910.

John Dos Passos. *U.S.A.: 1. The 42nd Parallel. 2. Nineteen Nineteen. 3. The Big Money.* New York: Harcourt, Brace, 1937.

W.E.B. Du Bois. *The Souls of Black Folk.* Chicago: A. C. McClurg, 1903.

Marguerite Duras. *L'amant {The Lover}.* Paris: Editions de minuit, 1984.

Emile Durkheim. *Le suicide: étude de sociologie {Suicide: A Study in Sociology}.* Paris: F. Alcan, 1897.

Albert Einstein. *The Meaning of Relativity: Four Lectures Delivered at Princeton University, May, 1921.* Translated by Edwin Plimpton Adams. London: Methuen, 1922.

T. S. Eliot. *The Waste Land.* New York: Boni and Liveright, 1922.

Havelock Ellis. *Studies in the Psychology of Sex.* 7 vols. Philadelphia: F. A. Davis, 1901–28.

Ralph Ellison. *Invisible Man.* New York: Random House, 1952.

Buchi Emecheta. *The Bride Price: A Novel.* London: Allison & Busby, 1976.

Frantz Fanon. *Les damnés de la terre {The Wretched of the Earth}.* Paris: F. Maspero, 1961.

William Faulkner. *The Portable Faulkner.* Edited by Malcolm Cowley. New York: Viking Press, 1946.

F. Scott Fitzgerald. *The Great Gatsby.* New York: Charles Scribner's Sons, 1925.

E. M. Forster. *A Passage to India.* London: Edward Arnold, 1924.

Anne Frank. *Het Achterhuis: Dagboekbrieven van 12 Juni 1942 – 1 Augustus 1944 {The Diary of a Young Girl}.* Amsterdam: Contact, 1947.

Sigmund Freud. *Die Traumdeutung {The Interpretation of Dreams}.* Leipzig and Vienna: F. Deuticke, 1900.

Betty Friedan. *The Feminine Mystique.* New York: Norton, 1963.

Milton Friedman. *A Theory of the Consumption Function.* Princeton: Princeton University Press, 1957.

John Kenneth Galbraith. *The Affluent Society.* Boston: Houghton Mifflin, 1958.

Mohandas K. Gandhi. *Satyagraha {Non-Violent Resistance}.* Ahmedabad: Navajivan Pub. House, 1951. {Collected edition of newspaper columns written 1921–40.}

Federico García Lorca. *Primer romancero gitano, 1924 – 1927 {Gypsy Ballads}.* Madrid: Revista de Occidente, 1928.

Gabriel García Márquez. *Cien años de soledad {One Hundred Years of Soli-*

tude}. (Colección Grandes novelas). Buenos Aires: Editorial Sud-america, 1967.

Kahlil Gibran. *The Prophet*. New York: Knopf, 1923.

Charlotte Perkins Gilman. *Herland*. First published in *The Forerunner*, 6 (1915). First monograph publication: New York: Pantheon, 1979.

Paul Goodman. *Growing Up Absurd: Problems of Youth in the Organized System*. New York: Random House, 1960.

Zane Grey. *Riders of the Purple Sage*. New York and London: Harper & Brothers, 1912.

Jaroslav Hašek. *Osudy dobrého vojáka Švejka za sv̆ětové války {The Good Soldier Schweik}*. 4 vols. Praha: A. Sauer a J. Hašek, 1920–23.

Friedrich A. Hayek. *The Road to Serfdom*. Foreword by John Chamberlain. Chicago: University of Chicago Press, 1944.

Robert A. Heinlein. *Stranger in a Strange Land*. New York: Putnam, 1961.

Joseph Heller. *Catch-22*. New York: Simon and Schuster, 1961.

Ernest Hemingway. *For Whom the Bell Tolls*. New York: Scribner, 1940.

Michael Herr. *Dispatches*. New York: Knopf, 1977.

John Hersey. *Hiroshima*. New York: Knopf, 1946.

Theodor Herzl. *Der Judenstaat: Versuch einer modernen Lösung der Judenfrage {The Jewish State}*. Leipzig and Vienna: M. Breitenstein, 1896.

James Hilton. *Lost Horizon*. London: Macmillan, 1933.

Adolf Hitler. *Mein Kampf: Eine Abrechnung*. 2 vols. Munich: F. Eher, 1925–26.

Langston Hughes. *The Best of Simple*. Illustrated by Bernhard Nast. New York: Hill and Wang, 1961.

Zora Neale Hurston. *Dust Tracks on a Road*. Philadelphia: Lippincott, 1942.

Aldous Huxley. *Brave New World*. Garden City, N.Y.: Doubleday, Doran, 1932.

Jane Jacobs. *The Death and Life of Great American Cities*. New York: Random House, 1961.

Henry James. *The Turn of the Screw*. In: *The Two Magics: The Turn of the Screw, Covering End*. New York and London: Macmillan, 1898.

William James. *The Varieties of Religious Experience: A Study in Human Nature*. New York and London: Longmans, Green, 1902.

Sarah Orne Jewett. *The Country of the Pointed Firs*. Boston and New York: Houghton, Mifflin, 1896.

Juan Ramón Jiménez. *Platero y yo {Platero and I; An Andalusian Elegy}*. Illustrated by Fernando Marco. Madrid: Ediciones de "La Lectura," 1914.

James Joyce. *Ulysses.* Paris: Shakespeare and Company, 1922.

Franz Kafka. *Die Verwandlung {The Metamorphosis}.* (Der Jüngste Tag. Bd. 22–23). Leipzig: K. Wolff, 1915.

Ryszard Kapuściński. *Cesarz {The Emperor}.* Warsaw: Czytelnik, ZG, 1978.

Ezra Jack Keats. *The Snowy Day.* New York: Viking Press, 1962.

Helen Keller. *The Story of My Life.* New York: Doubleday, Page, 1903.

Jack Kerouac. *On the Road.* New York: Viking Press, 1957.

Ken Kesey. *One Flew over the Cuckoo's Nest: A Novel.* New York: Viking Press, 1962.

John Maynard Keynes. *The General Theory of Employment, Interest and Money.* New York: Harcourt, Brace, 1936.

Stephen King. *Carrie.* New York: Doubleday, 1974.

Rudyard Kipling. *Kim.* London: Macmillan, 1901.

Arthur Koestler. *Darkness at Noon.* Translated by Daphne Hardy. New York: Macmillan, 1941.

Alex Kotlowitz. *There Are No Children Here: The Story of Two Boys Growing Up in the Other America.* New York: Doubleday, 1991.

Ed Krol. *The Whole Internet: User's Guide & Catalog.* Sebastopol, Calif.: O'Reilly & Associates, 1992.

Elisabeth Kübler-Ross. *On Death and Dying.* New York: Macmillan, 1969.

Timothy Leary. *The Politics of Ecstasy.* New York: Putnam, 1968.

Helen Leavitt. *Superhighway — Super Hoax.* Garden City, N.Y.: Doubleday, 1970.

Harper Lee. *To Kill a Mockingbird.* Philadelphia: Lippincott, 1960.

Aldo Leopold. *A Sand County Almanac, and Sketches Here and There.* New York: Oxford University Press, 1949.

Doris Lessing. *The Golden Notebook.* London: Michael Joseph, 1962.

C. S. Lewis. *The Lion, the Witch and the Wardrobe: A Story for Children.* Illustrated by Pauline Baynes. London: G. Bles, 1950.

Konrad Z. Lorenz. *Er redete mit dem Vieh, den Vögeln und den Fischen {King Solomon's Ring: New Light on Animal Ways}.* Vienna: Buchgemeinschaft Donauland, 1949.

Patricia MacLachlan. *Sarah, Plain and Tall.* New York: Harper & Row, 1985.

Maurice Maeterlinck. *La vie des abeilles {The Life of the Bee}.* Paris: E. Fasquelle, 1901.

Malcolm X. *The Autobiography of Malcolm X.* New York: Grove Press, 1965.

Thomas Mann. *Der Zauberberg: Roman {The Magic Mountain}.* Berlin: S. Fischer, 1924.

Mao Zedong. *Quotations from Chairman Mao.* Edited and printed by the Chinese People's Liberation Army, Political Department. Beijing, 1966.

Margaret Mead. *Coming of Age in Samoa.* New York: Morrow, 1928.

Rigoberta Menchú. *Me llamo Rigoberta Menchú y así me nació conciencia {I, Rigoberta Menchú}.* Barcelona: Argos Vergara, 1983.

Grace Metalious. *Peyton Place.* New York: Messner, 1956.

Edna St. Vincent Millay. *Renascence and Other Poems.* New York: M. Kennerley, 1917.

A. A. Milne. *Winnie-the-Pooh.* London: Methuen, 1926.

Margaret Mitchell. *Gone with the Wind.* New York: Macmillan, 1936.

Robin Morgan, editor. *Sisterhood Is Powerful: An Anthology of Writings from the Women's Liberation Movement.* New York: Random House, 1970.

Toni Morrison. *Song of Solomon.* New York: Knopf, 1977.

Vladimir Nabokov. *Lolita.* 2 vols. Paris: The Olympia Press, 1955.

V. S. Naipaul. *Guerrillas.* London: Deutsch, 1975.

George Orwell. *Nineteen Eighty-four.* London: Secker & Warburg, 1949.

Alan Paton. *Cry, the Beloved Country: A Story of Comfort in Desolation.* New York: Charles Scribner's Sons, 1948.

Roger Tory Peterson. *A Field Guide to the Birds: Giving Field Marks of All Species Found in Eastern North America.* Boston and New York: Houghton Mifflin, 1934.

Luigi Pirandello. *Sei personaggi in cerca d'autore {Six Characters in Search of an Author}.* (His Maschere nude, vol. 3). Florence: R. Bemporad, 1921.

Emily Post. *Etiquette in Society, in Business, in Politics, and at Home.* New York and London: Funk & Wagnalls, 1922.

Beatrix Potter. *The Tale of Peter Rabbit.* London: Strangeways, 1902.

Marcel Proust. *A la recherche du temps perdu {Remembrance of Things Past}.* 8 vols. Paris: Bernard Grasset (vol. 1); Editions de la Nouvelle Revue Française (vols. 2–8), 1913–27.

Ayn Rand. *Atlas Shrugged.* New York: Random House, 1957.

John Reed. *Ten Days That Shook the World.* New York: Boni and Liveright, 1919.

Erich Maria Remarque. *Im Westen nichts Neues {All Quiet on the Western Front}.* Berlin: Propyläen-Verlag, 1929.

Jean Rhys. *Wide Sargasso Sea.* London: Deutsch, 1966.

Jacob Riis. *The Battle with the Slum.* New York and London: Macmillan, 1902.

Irma S. Rombauer. *The Joy of Cooking: A Compilation of Reliable Recipes with a Casual Culinary Chat.* St. Louis: Privately printed, 1931.

Philip Roth. *Portnoy's Complaint.* New York: Random House, 1969.

Bertrand Russell. *Why I Am Not a Christian*. London: Watts, 1927.

Tayeb el-Salih. *Mawsim al-Hijra ila al-Shamal {Season of Migration to the North}*. Cairo: Dar al-Hilal, 1969.

J. D. Salinger. *The Catcher in the Rye*. Boston: Little, Brown, 1951.

Margaret Sanger. *My Fight for Birth Control*. New York: Farrar & Rinehart, 1931.

Jean-Paul Sartre. *L'être et le néant: essai d'ontologie phénoménologique {Being and Nothingness}*. Paris: Gallimard, 1943.

Siegfried Sassoon. *The War Poems*. London: Heinemann, 1919.

E. F. Schumacher. *Small Is Beautiful: A Study of Economics as if People Mattered*. New York: Harper & Row, 1973.

Maurice Sendak. *Where the Wild Things Are*. New York: Harper & Row, 1963.

Dr. Seuss. *The Cat in the Hat*. New York: Random House, 1957.

George Bernard Shaw. *Pygmalion*. London, 1914.

Randy Shilts. *And the Band Played On: Politics, People, and the AIDS Epidemic*. New York: St. Martin's Press, 1987.

Upton Sinclair. *The Jungle*. New York: Doubleday, Page, 1906.

B. F. Skinner. *Walden Two*. New York: Macmillan, 1948.

Betty Smith. *A Tree Grows in Brooklyn*. New York and London: Harper & Brothers, 1943.

Lillian Smith. *Strange Fruit*. New York: Reynal & Hitchcock, 1944.

Aleksandr I. Solzhenitsyn. *Arkhipelag GULag, 1918 – 1956 {The Gulag Archipelago, 1918 – 1956: An Experiment in Literary Investigation}*. Paris: YMCA-Press, 1973 – 75.

Art Spiegelman. *Maus: A Survivor's Tale*. 2 vols. New York: Pantheon Books, 1986–91.

Dr. Benjamin Spock. *The Common Sense Book of Baby and Child Care*. New York: Duell, Sloan and Pearce, 1946.

Lincoln Steffens. *The Autobiography of Lincoln Steffens*. 2 vols. New York: Harcourt, Brace, 1931.

Edward Steichen. *The Family of Man: The Photographic Exhibition Created by Edward Steichen for the Museum of Modern Art*. New York: Published for the Museum of Modern Art by Simon and Schuster, 1955.

Gertrude Stein. *Tender Buttons: Objects   Food   Rooms*. New York: Claire Marie, 1914.

John Steinbeck. *The Grapes of Wrath*. New York: Viking, 1939.

Bram Stoker. *Dracula*. Westminster: A. Constable, 1897.

Paul Tillich. *The Courage to Be*. New Haven: Yale University Press, 1952.

J.R.R. Tolkien. *The Hobbit*. London: Allen & Unwin, 1937.

Arnold Toynbee. *Armenian Atrocities: The Murder of a Nation.* London: Hodder & Stoughton, 1915.

United Nations. *Charter of the United Nations and Statute of the International Court of Justice.* San Francisco, 1945.

United States. Surgeon General's Advisory Committee on Smoking and Health. *Smoking and Health: Report of the Advisory Committee to the Surgeon General of the Public Health Service.* Washington, D.C.: U.S. Department of Health, Education, and Welfare, Public Health Service, 1964.

Thorstein Veblen. *The Theory of the Leisure Class: An Economic Study of Institutions.* New York: Macmillan, 1899.

Lillian Wald. *The House on Henry Street.* New York: Henry Holt, 1915.

Alice Walker. *The Color Purple: A Novel.* New York: Harcourt Brace Jovanovich, 1982.

James Watson. *The Double Helix: A Personal Account of the Discovery of the Structure of DNA.* New York: Atheneum, 1968.

Max Weber. *Die protestantische Ethik und der Geist des Kapitalismus {The Protestant Ethic and the Spirit of Capitalism}.* Tübingen and Leipzig: J.C.B. Mohr (P. Siebeck), 1904.

H. G. Wells. *The Time Machine.* London: Heinemann, 1895.

Nathanael West. *The Day of the Locust.* New York: Random House, 1939.

Edith Wharton. *The Age of Innocence.* New York and London: D. Appleton, 1920.

E. B. White. *Charlotte's Web.* Pictures by Garth Williams. New York: Harper & Row, 1952.

Elie Wiesel. *La nuit {Night}.* Foreword by François Mauriac. Paris: Editions de Minuit, 1958.

Edward O. Wilson. *The Diversity of Life.* Cambridge, Mass.: Belknap Press of Harvard University Press, 1992.

P. G. Wodehouse. *The Inimitable Jeeves.* London: H. Jenkins, 1923.

Tom Wolfe. *The Bonfire of the Vanities.* New York: Farrar Straus Giroux, 1987.

Virginia Woolf. *To the Lighthouse.* London: The Hogarth Press, 1927.

Richard Wright. *Native Son.* New York and London: Harper & Brothers, 1940.

William Butler Yeats. *The Wild Swans at Coole: Other Verses and a Play in Verse.* Churchtown, Dundrum: Cuala Press, 1917.

Notes

This list includes sources for quotations in the text, with the exception of quotations that come from the Books of the Century themselves.

LANDMARKS OF MODERN LITERATURE

p. 10: Richard Gilman, *The Making of Modern Drama: A Study of Büchner, Ibsen, Strindberg, Chekhov, Pirandello, Brecht, Beckett, Handke* (New York: Farrar, Straus & Giroux, 1974), p. 146.

p. 12: Sherwood Anderson, Foreword to Gertrude Stein, *Geography and Plays* (New York: Something Else Press, 1968), pp. 5, 8.

p. 14: Elizabeth P. Perlmutter, "A Doll's Heart: The Girl in the Poetry of Edna St. Vincent Millay and Louise Bogan," *Twentieth Century Literature*, 23, no. 2 (May 1977): 157.

p. 15: T. S. Eliot, "Yeats," in *Yeats: A Collection of Critical Essays*, ed. John Unterecker (Englewood Cliffs, N.J.: Prentice-Hall, 1963), p. 58.

p. 17: Edmund Wilson, *Axel's Castle: A Study in the Imaginative Literature of 1870 – 1930* (New York: Charles Scribner's Sons, 1943), pp. 106–14.

V. S. Pritchett, quoted in *Current Biography Yearbook 1962*, ed. Charles Moritz (New York: H. W. Wilson, 1962), p. 124.

p. 18: *United States v. One Book Called "Ulysses,"* 5 F. Supp. 182 (S.D.N.Y. 1933).

p. 19: Thomas Mann, "The Making of 'The Magic Mountain,' " *The Atlantic*, January 1953, pp. 41–45.

p. 20: Lionel Trilling, "F. Scott Fitzgerald," *The Liberal Imagination* (New York: Viking Press, 1950), p. 251.

p. 22: Federico García Lorca, *Deep Song and Other Prose*, ed. and trans.

Christopher Maurer (New York: New Directions, 1980), pp. 104–5.

p. 23:   Irving Howe, *A World More Attractive: A View of Modern Literature and Politics* (New York: Horizon Press, 1963), pp. 100–101.

David Bradley, "On Rereading *Native Son*," *The New York Times Book Review*, December 7, 1986, p. 79.

p. 26:   Brooks Atkinson, "Theatre: 'Godot' for Fair," *The New York Times*, August 6, 1958, p. 22.

p. 27:   Ralph Ellison, quoted in *Writers at Work: The* Paris Review *Interviews*, Second Series (New York: Viking Press, 1963), p. 322.

p. 29:   Donald Leslie Shaw, "Jorge Luis Borges: *Ficciones*," in *Landmarks in Modern Latin American Fiction*, ed. Philip Swanson (London and New York: Routledge, 1990), p. 34.

p. 33:   Toni Morrison, "Nobel Lecture 1993," *World Literature Today*, 68, no. 1 (Winter 1994): 7.

NATURE'S REALM

p. 38:   Bertrand Russell, *The ABC of Relativity*, revised edition, ed. Felix Pirani (London: George Allen & Unwin, 1958), p. 9.

PROTEST & PROGRESS

p. 47:   James Agee and Walker Evans, *Let Us Now Praise Famous Men: Three Tenant Families* (Boston: Houghton Mifflin, 1988), p. 15.

p. 50:   John Edgar Wideman, Foreword to W.E.B. Du Bois, *The Souls of Black Folk* (New York: Vintage Books/Library of America, 1990), p. xii.

p. 51:   Upton Sinclair, *American Outpost: A Book of Reminiscences* (New York: Farrar & Rinehart, Inc., 1932), pp. 166–69.

p. 54:   Theodore Roosevelt, "The Man with the Muck-rake," *The Works of Theodore Roosevelt* (New York: Charles Scribner's Sons, 1926), 16: 415.

p. 55:   Jean-Paul Sartre, *Literary and Philosophical Essays,* trans. Annette
           Michelson (New York: Criterion Books, 1955), p. 96.

p. 57:   "Experiment in Communication," *Time,* October 13, 1941, p.
           104.

p. 59:   "Paul Goodman, Author, Reformer, Iconoclast, Dies," *The
           New York Times,* August 4, 1972, p. 34.

p. 60:   Toni Morrison, "Life in His Language," *The New York Times
           Book Review,* December 20, 1987, p. 27.

p. 62:   Christopher Lehmann Haupt, "Books of the Times," *The New
           York Times,* October 26, 1987, p. C20.

p. 63:   Thomas Byrne Edsall, "The American Dilemma," *The New
           Republic,* 204, no. 21 (May 27, 1991): 36.

COLONIALISM & ITS AFTERMATH

p. 67:   Arthur Symons, *Notes on Joseph Conrad: With Some Unpublished
           Letters* (London: Myers & Co., 1925), p. 10.

p. 68:   Niraud C. Chaudhuri. "The Finest Story About India — In
           English," *Encounter,* 8, no. 4 (April 1957): 47.

           Bhupal Singh, *A Survey of Anglo Indian Fiction* (London: Oxford
           University Press, 1934), p. 79.

p. 69:   Mohandas K. Gandhi, *Young India: A Weekly Journal,* 11, no. 32
           (August 8, 1929): 263.

p. 70:   Martin Seymour-Smith, *The New Guide to Modern World Litera-
           ture* (New York: Peter Bedrick Books, 1985), p. 226.

p. 71:   Patrick McCarthy, *Camus* (New York: Random House, 1982), p. 9.

p. 73:   Alan Paton, *The Journey Continued: An Autobiography* (New
           York: Charles Scribner's Sons, 1988), p. 4.

p. 74:   Review in *The New Yorker,* September 17, 1955, p. 176.

p. 76:   *Time,* April 30, 1965, p. 114.

p. 78:   Saree S. Makdisi, "The Empire Renarrated: *Season of Migration
           to the North* and the Reinvention of the Present," *Critical
           Inquiry,* 18, no. 4 (Summer 1992): 807.

p. 79: Jane Kramer, "From the Third World," *The New York Times Book Review*, April 13, 1980, p. 1.

Paul Theroux, "An Intelligence from the Third World," *The New York Times Book Review*, November 16, 1975, p. 1.

p. 80: Review in *The New Yorker*, May 17, 1976, p. 171.

p. 82: *People*, December 21, 1992, pp. 87–88.

MIND & SPIRIT

p. 94: Robert Peel, *The Christian Science Monitor*, June 7, 1956, p. 7.

p. 97: Paul Tillich, quoted in the *New York Post*, May 1, 1940, p. 13.

Rollo May, *Paulus: Reminiscences of a Friendship* (New York: Harper & Row, 1973), pp. 82–83.

POPULAR CULTURE & MASS ENTERTAINMENT

p. 104: Anthony Boucher, Introduction in Bram Stoker, *Dracula: With an Introduction by Anthony Boucher: Illustrated with Wood Engravings by Felix Hoffmann* (New York: Limited Editions Club, 1965), p. ix.

p. 107: Ray Bradbury, "Introduction: Tarzan, John Carter, Mr. Burroughs, and the Long Mad Summer of 1930," in Irwin Porges, *Edgar Rice Burroughs: The Man Who Created Tarzan* (Provo: Brigham Young University Press, 1975), p. xix.

p. 112: Raymond Chandler, "The Simple Art of Murder," *Atlantic Monthly*, 174, no. 6 (December 1944): 59.

p. 113: Clifton Fadiman, review in *The New Yorker*, May 20, 1939, pp. 91–92.

p. 114: Carlos Baker, "Small Town Peep Show," *The New York Times Book Review*, September 23, 1956, p. 4.

p. 118: Conrad Knickerbocker, "One Night on a Kansas Farm," *The New York Times Book Review*, January 16, 1966, p. 1.

p. 121: Jonathan Yardley, "Tom Wolfe's New York Confidential,"

Washington Post Book World, October 25, 1987, p. 3.

p. 121: Nicholas Lemann, "New York in the Eighties," *The Atlantic,* 260, no. 6 (December 1987): 106.

WOMEN RISE

p. 125: Margaret B. McDowell, quoted in *"The Age of Innocence:* Edith Wharton," *Twentieth Century Literary Criticism,* vol. 53, ed. Laurie Di Mauro (Detroit: Gale Research, 1994), p. 361.

p. 127: Margaret Sanger, *An Autobiography* (New York: W. W. Norton & Company, 1938), p. 87.

p. 128: Langston Hughes, *The Big Sea* (New York & London: Alfred A. Knopf, 1945), p. 239.

p. 129: Ellen Willis, quoted in "Simone de Beauvoir," *Contemporary Literary Criticism,* vol. 71, ed. Thomas Votteler (Detroit: Gale Research, 1992), p. 36.

p. 130: Pearl K. Bell, "Bad Housekeeping," *The New Republic,* October 28, 1985, p. 47.

p. 135: Alice Walker, quoted in Derrick Bell, "The Word from Alice Walker," *The Los Angeles Times Book Review,* May 29, 1988, p. 11.

ECONOMICS & TECHNOLOGY

p. 139: Alfred Kazin, *On Native Grounds: An Interpretation of Modern American Prose Literature* (New York: Harcourt, Brace & World, 1942), p. 137.

John Kenneth Galbraith, "Introduction: Thorstein Veblen and *The Theory of the Leisure Class,*" in Thorstein Veblen, *The Theory of the Leisure Class* (Boston: Houghton Mifflin Company, 1973), p. xvii.

p. 142: Warren J. Samuels, "John Maynard Keynes," *Thinkers of the Twentieth Century,* second edition, ed. Roland Turner (Chicago and London: St. James Press, 1987), p. 403.

p. 148: Martin Mayer, "The Closet Conservatives," *The American Scholar,* 46 (Spring 1977): 233.

p. 149: "About the Author," in Ed Krol, *The Whole Internet: User's Guide & Catalog* (Sebastopol, Calif.: O'Reilly & Associates, 1992), p. 377.

UTOPIAS & DYSTOPIAS

p. 154: Ernst Pawel, *The Labyrinth of Exile: A Life of Theodor Herzl* (New York: Farrar, Straus & Giroux, 1989), p. 467.

p. 156: Peter Llewelyn Davies, quoted in Janet Dunbar, *J. M. Barrie: The Man Behind the Image* (Boston: Houghton Mifflin, 1970), p. 165.

p. 157: P. L. Adams, review in *The Atlantic,* April 1979, p. 99.

p. 158: Peter Edgerly Firchow, *The End of Utopia: A Study of Aldous Huxley's* Brave New World (Lewisburg: Bucknell University Press, 1984), p. 9.

p. 163: Claudia Roth Pierpont, "Twilight of the Goddess," *The New Yorker,* July 24, 1995, p. 70.

p. 165: John Updike, review in *The New Yorker,* May 12, 1986, p. 121.

WAR, HOLOCAUST, TOTALITARIANISM

p. 169: V. I. Lenin, Introduction to John Reed, *Ten Days That Shook the World* (New York: International Publishers, 1919).

Max Eastman, *Heroes I Have Known: Twelve Who Lived Great Lives* (New York: Simon & Schuster, 1942), p. 201.

p. 172: Winston Churchill, *The Gathering Storm.* Volume 1 of *The Second World War* (Boston: Houghton Mifflin, 1948), p. 55.

p. 174: Joseph Brodsky, *Less Than One: Selected Essays* (New York: Farrar, Straus & Giroux, 1986), p. 52.

p. 175: Philip Young, *Ernest Hemingway: A Reconsideration* (University Park: Pennsylvania State University Press, 1966), pp. 200–201.

p. 176: George Orwell, review in *The New Statesman and Nation,* 21, no. 515 (January 4, 1941): 16.

p. 178: Lies Goslar Pick, as told to Stanley Frank, "I Knew Anne Frank," *McCall's,* July 1958, p. 115.

p. 180: A. Alvarez, *Beyond All This Fiddle* (London: Allen Lane, The Penguin Press, 1968), p. 23.

p. 184: C.D.B. Bryan, "The Different War," *The New York Times Book Review,* November 20, 1977, p. 1.

Paul Gray, "Secret History," *Time,* November 7, 1977, p. 120.

p. 185: Lawrence L. Langer, "A Fable of the Holocaust," *The New York Times Book Review,* November 3, 1991, p. 36.

OPTIMISM, JOY, GENTILITY

p. 186: Robert Frost, "The Figure a Poem Makes," in *Robert Frost: Poetry & Prose,* ed. Edward Connery Lathem and Lawrance Thompson (New York: Holt, Rinehart and Winston, 1972), p. 394.

p. 189: Francis Otto Matthiessen, *Sarah Orne Jewett* (Boston and New York: Houghton Mifflin Company, 1929), p. 151.

p. 191: G. K. Chesterton, *The Autobiography of G. K. Chesterton* (New York: Sheed & Ward, 1936), pp. 333–34.

p. 192: Michael P. Predmore, "The Structure of *Platero y Yo,*" *PMLA: Publications of the Modern Language Society of America,* 85, no. 1 (January 1970): 56, 58.

p. 193: David J. Gordon, *Bernard Shaw and the Comic Sublime* (Basingstoke: Macmillan, 1990), pp. 146–47.

p. 195: Evelyn Waugh, "An Act of Homage and Reparation to P. G. Wodehouse," *The Essays, Articles and Reviews of Evelyn Waugh*, ed. Donat Gallagher (London: Methuen, 1983), p. 567.

p. 199: C. S. Lewis, "The Gods Return to Earth," *Time & Tide: The Independent Weekly,* 35, no. 33 (August 14, 1954): 1083.

p. 200: Margaret Wise Brown, quoted in Louise Seaman Bechtel,

"Margaret Wise Brown, 'Laureate of the Nursery,'" *The Horn Book Magazine,* 34, no. 3 (June 1958): 186.

p. 202: Richard Barksdale and Keneth Kinnamon, *Black Writers of America: A Comprehensive Anthology* (New York: The Macmillan Company, 1972), p. 517.

p. 203: Octavio Paz, "Elizabeth Bishop, or the Power of Reticence," *World Literature Today,* 51, no. 1 (Winter 1977): 15.

FAVORITES OF CHILDHOOD AND YOUTH

p. 206: Anne Carroll Moore, "An Appreciation," in Beatrix Potter, *The Art of Beatrix Potter: With an Appreciation by Anne Carroll Moore* (London and New York: F. Warne, 1955), p. 13.

Maurice Sendak, *Caldecott & Co.: Notes on Books and Pictures* (New York: Farrar, Straus & Giroux, 1988), p. 76.

p. 207: "Betty Smith, Author, Dies at 75; Wrote 'Tree Grows in Brooklyn,'" *The New York Times,* January 18, 1972, p. 34.

Orville Prescott, review in *Yale Review,* 33, no. 1 (Autumn 1943): viii.

p. 208: Roger Lancelyn Green, *Tellers of Tales* (Leicester, England: E. Ward, 1953), p. 259.

p. 209: Virgilia Peterson, review in *The New York Herald Tribune Book Review,* July 15, 1951, p. 3.

p. 210: Eudora Welty, "Life in the Barn Was Very Good," *The New York Times Book Review,* October 19, 1952, p. 49.

p. 211: Lee Bennett Hopkins, *Books Are by People: Interviews with 104 Authors and Illustrators of Books for Young Children* (New York: Citation Press, 1969), p. 104.

p. 212: Maurice Sendak, *Caldecott & Co.: Notes on Books and Pictures* (New York: Farrar, Straus & Giroux, 1988), p. 146.

p. 213: Ethel L. Heins, review in *The Horn Book Magazine,* 61, no. 5 (September/October 1985): 558.

Patricia MacLachlan, "Newbery Medal Acceptance," *The Horn Book Magazine,* 62, no. 4 (July/August 1986): 412.

A Note About the Artist

The illustrations in this book were created by internationally known artist Diana Bryan originally as large wall murals for the Library's exhibition *Books of the Century*. The murals measure horizontally between 10' and 32' each, and were made by a unique process in which paper cut-outs were photostatically enlarged into murals.

Ms. Bryan is a member of the faculty of Parsons School of Design, and is a published illustrator whose work has appeared in *The New York Times*, *The Wall Street Journal*, *Rolling Stone*, *Ms.*, *The Village Voice*, and *The New Yorker*. Other clients include The Public Theater, AT&T, IBM, Time-Life Books, Walden Books, Doubleday, and many others.

Diana Bryan has produced two children's videos for Rabbit Ears, both of which have won awards: *The Fisherman and His Wife*, narrated by Jodie Foster, winner of the Parent's Choice Honor Award; and *The Monkey People*, narrated by Raul Julia, winner of the Texas International Animation Festival Gold Award. Two companion children's books, both published by Simon & Schuster, are available with the videos. Both videos have been shown on the HBO and Showtime cable television networks.

Books of the Century Project Team

The exhibition *Books of the Century* was on view in the Third Floor Galleries at the Center for the Humanities from May 20, 1995 through July 13, 1996.

Curator: Elizabeth Diefendorf, the Frederick Phineas and Sandra Priest Rose Chief Librarian of the General Research Division

Project Manager: Karen Van Westering, Manager of Publications

Illustrations: Diana Bryan

Writing and Editorial Assistance: Nina Sonenberg, Anne Skillion, Barbara Bergeron

Exhibitions Staff:

Susan Rabbiner, Assistant Manager

Myriam de Arteni, Conservator

Jeanne Bornstein, Research Coordinator

Polly Hubbard, Education Coordinator

Jean Mihich, Registrar

Lou Storey, Exhibition Designer

Barbara Suhr, Assistant Designer

Todd Sowers, Exhibitions Assistant

Laura Howell, Exhibition Graphics

Susanna Stieff, Exhibition Graphics

Art Handlers: Anne Burton, Susan Fisher, Maddine Isalaco, Honor Mosher, Judith Ribicoff, Erik Zuber

Assistant Registrars: Kenneth Doyle, Bradford Johnson

Centennial Exhibitions:

Marie Salerno, Vice President for Public Affairs

David Cronin, Manager, Public Programs

Centennial Development:

Bonnie Levinson, Vice President for Development

Karen Pratt, Associate Manager, Corporate Relations & Special Campaigns